Praise for *Scalability*

P9-EDE-728

"Once again, Abbott and Fisher provide a book that I'll be giving
to our engineers. It's an essential read for anyone dealing with
scaling an online business."

> —**Chris Lalonde**, VP, Technical Operations and Infrastructure
> Architecture, Bullhorn

"Abbott and Fisher again tackle the difficult problem of scalability
in their unique and practical manner. Distilling the challenges of
operating a fast-growing presence on the Internet into 50 easy-to-
understand rules, the authors provide a modern cookbook of
scalability recipes that guide the reader through the difficulties
of fast growth."

> —**Geoffrey Weber**, Vice President, Internet Operations, Shutterfly

"Abbott and Fisher have distilled years of wisdom into a set of
cogent principles to avoid many nonobvious mistakes."

> —**Jonathan Heiliger**, VP, Technical Operations, Facebook

"In *The Art of Scalability*, the AKF team taught us that scale is not
just a technology challenge. Scale is obtained only through a
combination of people, process, *and* technology. With *Scalability
Rules*, Martin Abbott and Michael Fisher fill our scalability toolbox
with easily implemented and time-tested rules that once applied
will enable massive scale."

> —**Jerome Labat**, VP, Product Development IT, Intuit

"When I joined Etsy, I partnered with Mike and Marty to hit the
ground running in my new role, and it was one of the best
investments of time I have made in my career. The indispensable
advice from my experience working with Mike and Marty is fully
captured here in this book. Whether you're taking on a role as a
technology leader in a new company or you simply want to make
great technology decisions, *Scalability Rules* will be the go-to
resource on your bookshelf."

> —**Chad Dickerson**, CTO, Etsy

"*Scalability Rules* provides an essential set of practical tools and concepts anyone can use when designing, upgrading, or inheriting a technology platform. It's very easy to focus on an immediate problem and overlook issues that will appear in the future. This book ensures strategic design principles are applied to everyday challenges."

—**Robert Guild**, Director and Senior Architect, Financial Services

"An insightful, practical guide to designing and building scalable systems. A must-read for both product building and operations teams, this book offers concise and crisp insights gained from years of practical experience of AKF principals. With the complexity of modern systems, scalability considerations should be an integral part of the architecture and implementation process. Scaling systems for hypergrowth requires an agile, iterative approach that is closely aligned with product features; this book shows you how."

—**Nanda Kishore**, Chief Technology Officer, ShareThis

"For organizations looking to scale technology, people, and processes rapidly or effectively, the twin pairing of *Scalability Rules* and *The Art of Scalability* are unbeatable. The rules-driven approach in *Scalability Rules* makes this not only an easy reference companion, but also allows organizations to tailor the Abbott and Fisher approach to their specific needs both immediately and in the future!"

—**Jeremy Wright**, CEO, BNOTIONS.ca and Founder, b5media

Scalability
Rules

*50 Principles for
Scaling Web Sites*

Martin L. Abbott
Michael T. Fisher

♦♦Addison-Wesley

Upper Saddle River, NJ • Boston • Indianapolis • San Francisco
New York • Toronto • Montreal • London • Munich • Paris • Madrid
Cape Town • Sydney • Tokyo • Singapore • Mexico City

Many of the designations used by manufacturers and sellers to distinguish their products are claimed as trademarks. Where those designations appear in this book, and the publisher was aware of a trademark claim, the designations have been printed with initial capital letters or in all capitals.

The authors and publisher have taken care in the preparation of this book, but make no expressed or implied warranty of any kind and assume no responsibility for errors or omissions. No liability is assumed for incidental or consequential damages in connection with or arising out of the use of the information or programs contained herein.

The publisher offers excellent discounts on this book when ordered in quantity for bulk purchases or special sales, which may include electronic versions and/or custom covers and content particular to your business, training goals, marketing focus, and branding interests. For more information, please contact:

U.S. Corporate and Government Sales
(800) 382-3419
corpsales@pearsontechgroup.com

For sales outside the United States, please contact:

International Sales
international@pearson.com

Visit us on the Web: informit.com/aw

Library of Congress Cataloging-in-Publication Data:

Abbott, Martin L.
  Scalability rules : 50 principles for scaling Web sites
/ Martin L. Abbott, Michael T. Fisher.
     p. cm.
  ISBN 978-0-321-75388-5 (pbk. : alk. paper) — ISBN
(invalid) 01321753887 (pbk. : alk. paper) 1.
Computer networks—Scalability. 2. Web sites—
Security measures. I. Fisher, Michael T. II. Title.
  TK5105.59.A23 2011
  006.7—dc22

                               2011006257

Pearson Education, Inc
Rights and Contracts Department
501 Boylston Street, Suite 900
Boston, MA 02116
Fax (617) 671 3447

ISBN-13: 978-0-321-75388-5
ISBN-10: 0-321-75388-7

Text printed in the United States on recycled paper at R.R. Donnelley in Crawfordsville, Indiana.
First printing May 2011

Editor-in-Chief
Mark Taub

Senior Acquisitions Editor
Trina MacDonald

Development Editor
Songlin Qiu

Managing Editor
Kristy Hart

Project Editor
Anne Goebel

Copy Editor
Geneil Breeze

Indexer
Erika Millen

Proofreader
Linda Seifert

Technical Reviewers
Robert Guild
Geoffrey Weber
Jeremy Wright

Publishing Coordinator
Olivia Basegio

Cover Designer
Chuti Prasertsith

Senior Compositor
Gloria Schurick

❖

This book is dedicated to our
friend and partner
"Big" Tom Keeven.
"Big" refers to the impact he's
had in helping countless
companies scale in his nearly
30 years in the business.

❖

Contents at a Glance

Preface

Thanks for your interest in *Scalability Rules*! This book is meant to serve as a primer, a refresher, and a lightweight reference manual to help engineers, architects, and managers develop and maintain scalable Internet products. It is laid out in a series of rules, each of them bundled thematically by different topics. Most of the rules are technically focused, while a smaller number of them address some critical mindset or process concern— each of which is absolutely critical to building scalable products. The rules vary in their depth and focus. Some rules are high level, such as defining a model that can be applied to nearly any scalability problem, while others are specific and may explain a technique, such as how to modify headers to maximize the "cache-ability" of content.

Quick Start Guide

For experienced engineers, architects, and managers read through the header sections of all the rules that contain the what, when, how, and why. You can browse through each chapter reading these, or you can jump to Chapter 13, "Rule Review and Prioritization," which has a consolidated view of these headers. Once you've read these go back to the chapters that are new to you or that you find more interesting.

For less experienced readers we understand that 50 rules can seem overwhelming. We do believe that you should eventually become familiar with all the rules, but we also understand that you need to prioritize your time. With that in mind, we have picked out five chapters for managers, five chapters for software developers, and five chapters for technical operations that we recommend you read before the others to get a jump start on your scalability knowledge.

Managers:

- Chapter 1, "Reduce the Equation"
- Chapter 2, "Distribute Your Work"
- Chapter 4, "Use the Right Tools"
- Chapter 7, "Learn from Your Mistakes"
- Chapter 12, "Miscellaneous Rules"

Software developers:

- Chapter 1, "Reduce the Equation"
- Chapter 2, "Distribute Your Work"
- Chapter 5, "Don't Duplicate Your Work"
- Chapter 10, "Avoid or Distribute State"
- Chapter 11, "Asynchronous Communication and Message Buses"

Technical operations:

- Chapter 2, "Distribute Your Work"
- Chapter 3, "Design to Scale Out Horizontally"
- Chapter 6, "Use Caching Aggressively"
- Chapter 8, "Database Rules"
- Chapter 9, "Design for Fault Tolerance and Graceful Failure"

As you have time later, we recommend reading all the rules to familiarize yourself with the rules and concepts that we present no matter what your role. The book is short and can probably be read in a coast-to-coast flight in the US.

After the first read, the book can be used as a reference. If you are looking to fix or re-architect an existing product, Chapter 13, "Rule Review and Prioritization," offers an approach to applying the rules to your existing platform based on cost and the expected benefit (presented as a reduction of risk). If you already have your own prioritization mechanism, we do not recommend changing it for ours unless you like our approach better. If you don't have an existing method of prioritization, then our method should help you think through which rules you should apply first.

If you are just starting to develop a new product, the rules can help inform and guide you as to best practices for scaling. In this case, the approach of prioritization represented in Chapter 13 can best be used as a guide to what's most important to consider in your design. You should look at the rules that are most likely to allow you to scale for your immediate and long-term needs and implement those.

For all organizations, the rules can serve to help you create a set of architectural principles to drive future development. Select the 5, 10, or 15 rules that will help your product scale best and use them as an augmentation to your existing design reviews. Engineers and architects can ask questions relevant to each of the scalability rules that you select and ensure that any new significant design meets your scalability standards. While these rules are as specific and fixed as possible there is room for modification based on your system's particular criteria. If you or your team has extensive scalability experience, go ahead and tweak these rules as necessary to fit your particular scenario. If you and your team are lacking large scale experience use them exactly as is and see how far they allow you to scale.

Finally, this book is meant to serve as a reference and handbook. Chapter 13 is set up as a quick reference and summary of the rules. Whether you are experiencing problems or simply looking to develop a more scalable solution, Chapter 13 can become a quick reference guide to help pinpoint the rules that will help you out of your predicament fastest or help you define the best path forward in the event of new development. Besides using this as a desktop reference also consider integrating this into your organization by one of many tactics such as taking one or two rules each week and discussing them at your technology all-hands meeting.

Why Write Another Book on Scale?

There simply aren't many good books on scalability on the market yet, and *Scalability Rules* is unique in its approach in this sparse market. It is the first book to address the topic of scalability in a rules-oriented fashion. It is the first book meant to be as much of a reference as it is an overview of the topic. It includes a chapter summarizing the 50 rules and gives a prioritization of the rules for those looking to apply the book to their existing platforms.

One of our most-commented-on blog posts is on the need for scalability to become a discipline. We and the community of technologists that tackle scalability problems believe that scalability architects are needed in today's technology organizations. In the early days of computer systems almost everyone involved was a programmer, and then came specialization with system operators, DBAs, architects, and so on. We now have many different disciplines and specialties that make up our technology teams. One of the missing disciplines is the scalability architect.

Unlike a DBA, whose job is to get things done and not necessarily teach someone else unless they are mentoring a junior DBA, one of the primary responsibilities of the scalability architect would be to educate technology people. The scalability architects should be evangelists and teachers rather than the gatekeepers of secret knowledge. As part of that teaching we've made a step forward by putting together these 50 rules that we believe will help guide any organization in scaling its systems.

How Did You Decide What 50 Rules to Include?

The decision of which rules to include wasn't easy. This could easily be a book of 100 or even 200 rules. Our criteria for inclusion was to look at the recommendations that we make most often to our client base and find the most commonly recommended changes, additions, or modifications to their products. When we looked at these rules, we saw a fairly sharp drop-off in the rate of recommendations after the first 50 rules. That's not to say that we made these 50 recommendations equally, or that the 51st potential rule wasn't also fairly common. Rather, these 50 were just recommended more often with our clients. The rules aren't presented in order of frequency of recommendation. In Chapter, 13 we group the rules by their benefit and priority based on how we ranked each rule's risk reduction and cost of implementation or adoption.

How Does *Scalability Rules* Differ from *The Art of Scalability*?

The Art of Scalability (ISBN: 0137030428, published by Addison-Wesley), our first book on this topic, focused on people, process, and technology, while *Scalability Rules* is predominately a technically focused book. Don't get us wrong, we still believe that people and process are the most important component of build-ing scalable solutions. After all, it's the organization, including both the individual contributors and the management, which succeeds or fails in producing scalable solutions. The technology isn't at fault for failing to scale—it's the people who are at fault for building it, selecting it, or integrating it. But we believe that *The Art of Scalability* adequately addresses the people and process concerns around scalability, and we wanted to go in greater depth on the technical aspects of scalability.

Scalability Rules expands on the third (technical) section of our first book. The material in *Scalability Rules* is either new or discussed in a more technical fashion than in *The Art of Scalability*. Where we discussed something in that book, we expand upon it or define it in a slightly different way to help readers better understand the concept.

Acknowledgments

The rules contained within this book weren't developed by our partnership alone. They are the result of nearly 60 years of work with clients, colleagues, and partners within nearly 200 companies, divisions, and organizations. Each of them contributed, in varying degrees, to some or all of the rules within this book. As such, we would like to acknowledge the contributions of our friends, partners, clients, coworkers, and bosses for whom or with which we've worked over the past several (combined) decades.

We would also like to acknowledge and thank the editors who have provided guidance, feedback, and project management. Our technical editors Geoffrey Weber, Jeremy Wright, and Robert Guild shared with us their combined decades of technology experience and provided invaluable insight. Our editors from Addison-Wesley, Songlin Qiu and Trina MacDonald, provided supportive stylistic and rhetorical guidance throughout every step of this project. Thank you all for helping with this project.

Last but certainly not least we'd like to thank our families and friends who put up with our absence from social events to sit in front of a computer screen and write. No undertaking of this magnitude is done single-handedly, and without our families' and friends' understanding and support this would have been a much more arduous journey.

About the Authors

Martin L. Abbott is an executive with experience running technology and business organizations within Fortune 500 and startup companies. He is a founding partner of AKF Partners, a consulting firm focusing on meeting the technical and business hyper growth needs of today's fast-paced companies. Marty was formerly the COO of Quigo, an advertising technology startup acquired by AOL in 2007, where he was responsible for product strategy, product management, technology development, advertising, and publisher services. Prior to Quigo, Marty spent nearly six years at eBay, most recently as SVP of Technology and CTO and member of the CEO's executive staff. Prior to eBay, Marty held domestic and international engineering, management, and executive positions at Gateway and Motorola. Marty serves on the boards of directors for OnForce, LodgeNet Interactive (NASD:LNET), and Bullhorn. He sits on a number of advisory boards for universities and public and private companies. Marty has a BS in computer science from the United States Military Academy, an MS in computer engineering from the University of Florida, is a graduate of the Harvard Business School Executive Education Program, and is pursuing a Doctorate of Management from Case Western Reserve University. His current research investigates the antecedents and effects of conflict within executive teams of startups.

Michael T. Fisher is a veteran software and technology executive with experience in both Fortune 500 and startup companies. "Fish" is a founding partner of AKF Partners, a consulting firm focusing on meeting the technical and business hyper growth needs of today's fast-paced companies. Michael's experience includes two years as the chief technology officer of Quigo, a startup Internet advertising company acquired by AOL in 2007. Prior to Quigo, Michael served as vice president of engineering & architecture for PayPal, Inc., an eBay company. Prior to joining PayPal, Michael spent seven years at General Electric helping to develop the company's technology strategy and processes. Michael served six years as a captain and pilot in the

US Army. He sits on a number of boards of directors and advisory boards for private and nonprofit companies. Michael has a BS in computer science from the United States Military Academy, an MSIS from Hawaii Pacific University, a Ph.D. in Information Systems from Kennedy-Western University, and an MBA from Case Western Reserve University. Michael is a certified Six Sigma Master Black Belt and is pursuing a Doctorate of Management from Case Western Reserve University. His current research investigates the drivers for the viral growth of digital services.

1

Reduce the Equation

We've all been there at some point in our academic or professional careers: We stare at a complex problem and begin to lose hope. Where do we begin? How can we possibly solve the problem within the allotted time? Or in the extreme case—how do we solve it within a single lifetime? There's just too much to do, the problem is too complex, and it simply can't be solved. That's it. Pack it in. Game over...

Hold on—don't lose hope! Take a few deep breaths and channel your high school or college math teacher/professor. If you have a big hairy architectural problem, do the same thing you would do with a big hairy math equation and reduce it into easily solvable parts. Break off a small piece of the problem and break it into several smaller problems until each of the problems is easily solvable!

Our view is that any big problem, if approached properly, is really just a collection of smaller problems waiting to be solved. This chapter is all about making big architectural problems smaller and doing less work while still achieving the necessary business results. In many cases this approach actually reduces (rather than increases) the amount of work necessary to solve the problem, simplify the architecture and the solution, and end up with a much more scalable solution or platform.

As is the case with many of the chapters in *Scalability Rules*, the rules vary in size and complexity. Some are overarching rules easily applied to several aspects of our design. Some rules are very granular and prescriptive in their implementation to specific systems.

Rule 1—Don't Overengineer the Solution

> **Rule 1: What, When, How, and Why**
>
> **What:** Guard against complex solutions during design.
>
> **When to use:** Can be used for any project and should be used for all large or complex systems or projects.
>
> **How to use:** Resist the urge to overengineer solutions by testing ease of understanding with fellow engineers.
>
> **Why:** Complex solutions are costly to implement and have excessive long-term costs.
>
> **Key takeaways:** Systems that are overly complex limit your ability to scale. Simple systems are more easily and cost effectively maintained and scaled.

As Wikipedia explains, overengineering falls into two broad categories.[1] The first category covers products designed and implemented to exceed the useful requirements of the product. We discuss this problem briefly for completeness, but in our estimation its impact to scale is small compared to the second problem. The second category of overengineering covers products that are made to be overly complex. As we earlier implied, we are most concerned about the impact of this second category to scalability. But first, let's address the notion of exceeding requirements.

To explain the first category of overengineering, the exceeding of useful requirements, we must first make sense of the term *useful*, which here means simply capable of being used. For example, designing an HVAC unit for a family house that is capable of heating that house to 300 degrees Fahrenheit in outside temperatures of 0 Kelvin simply has no use for us anywhere. The effort necessary to design and manufacture such a solution is wasted as compared to a solution that might heat the house to a comfortable living temperature in environments where outside temperatures might get close to −20 degrees Fahrenheit. This type of overengineering might have cost overrun elements, including a higher cost to develop (engineer) the solution and a higher cost to implement the solution in hardware and software. It may further impact the company by delaying the product launch if the overengineered system took longer to develop than the useful system. Each of these costs has stakeholder impact as higher costs result in lower margins, and longer development times result in delayed revenue or benefits. *Scope creep*, or the addition of scope between initial product definition and initial product launch, is one manifestation of overengineering.

An example closer to our domain of experience might be developing an employee timecard system capable of handling a number of employees for a single company that equals or exceeds 100 times the population of Planet Earth. The probability that the Earth's population increases 100-fold within the useful life of the software is tiny. The possibility that all of those people work for a single company is even smaller. We certainly want to build our systems to scale to customer demands, but we don't want to waste time implementing and deploying those capabilities too far ahead of our need (see Rule 2).

The second category of overengineering deals with making something overly complex and making something in a complex way. Put more simply, the second category consists of either making something work harder to get a job done than is necessary, making a user work harder to get a job done than is necessary, or making an engineer work harder to understand something than is necessary. Let's dive into each of these three areas of overly complex systems.

What does it mean to make something work harder than is necessary? Some of the easiest examples come from the real world. Imagine that you ask your significant other to go to the grocery store. When he agrees, you tell him to pick up one of everything at the store, and then to pause and call you when he gets to the checkout line. Once he calls, you will tell him the handful of items that you would like from the many baskets of items he has collected and he can throw everything else on the floor. "Don't be ridiculous!" you might say. But have you ever performed a `select (*) from schema_name. table_name` SQL statement within your code only to cherry-pick your results from the returned set (see Rule 35)? Our grocery store example is essentially the same activity as the select (*) case above. How many lines of conditionals have you added to your code to handle edge cases and in what order are they evaluated? Do you handle the most likely case first? How often do you ask your database to return a result set you just returned, and how often do you re-create an HTML page you just displayed? This particular problem (doing work repetitively when you can just go back and get your last correct answer) is so rampant and easily overlooked that we've dedicated an entire chapter (Chapter 6, "Use Caching Aggressively") to this topic! You get the point.

What do we mean by making a user work harder than is necessary? The answer to this one is really pretty simple. In many cases, less is more. Many times in the pursuit of trying to make a system flexible, we strive to cram as many odd features as possible into it. Variety is not always the spice of life. Many times users just want to get from point A to point B as quickly as possible without distractions. If 99% of your market doesn't care about being able to save their blog as a .pdf file, don't build in a prompt asking them if they'd like to save it as a .pdf. If your users are interested in converting .wav files to mp3 files, they are already sold on a loss of fidelity, so don't distract them with the ability to convert to lossless compression FLAC files.

Finally we come to the notion of making software complex to understand for other engineers. Back in the day it was all the rage, and in fact there were competitions, to create complex code that would be difficult for others to understand. Sometimes this complex code would serve a purpose—it would run faster than code developed by the average engineer. More often than not the code complexity (in terms of ability to understand what it was doing due rather than a measure like cyclomatic complexity) would simply be an indication of one's "brilliance" or mastery of "kung fu." Medals were handed out for the person who could develop code that would bring senior developers to tears of acquiescence within code reviews. Complexity became the intellectual cage within which geeky code-slingers would battle for organizational dominance. It was a great game for those involved, but companies and shareholders were the ones paying for the tickets for a cage match no one cares about. For those interested in continuing in the geek fest, but in a "safe room" away from the potential stakeholder value destruction of doing it "for real," we suggest you partake in the International Obfuscated C Code Contest at www0.us.ioccc.org/main.html.

We should all strive to write code that everyone can understand. The real measure of a great engineer is how quickly that engineer can simplify a complex problem (see Rule 3) and develop an easily understood and maintainable solution. Easy to follow solutions mean that less senior engineers can more quickly come up to speed to support systems. Easy to understand solutions mean that problems can be found more quickly during troubleshooting, and systems can be restored to their proper working order in a faster manner. Easy to follow solutions increase the scalability of your organization and your solution.

A great test to determine whether something is too complex is to have the engineer in charge of solving a given complex problem present his or her solution to several engineering cohorts within the company. The cohorts should represent different engineering experience levels as well as varying tenures within the company (we make a difference here because you might have experienced engineers with very little company experience). To pass this test, each of the engineering cohorts should easily understand the solution, and each cohort should be able to describe the solution, unassisted, to others not otherwise knowledgeable about the solution. If any cohort does not understand the solution, the team should debate whether the system is overly complex.

Overengineering is one of the many enemies of scale. Developing a solution beyond that which is useful simply wastes money and time. It may further waste processing resources, increase the cost of scale, and limit the overall scalability of the system (how far that system can be scaled). Building solutions that are overly complex has a similar effect. Systems that work too hard increase your cost and limit your ultimate size. Systems that make users work too hard limit how quickly you are likely to increase users and therefore how quickly you will grow your business. Systems that are too complex to understand kill organizational productivity and the ease with which you can add engineers or add functionality to your system.

Rule 2—Design Scale into the Solution (D-I-D Process)

> **Rule 2: What, When, How, and Why**
>
> **What:** An approach to provide JIT (Just In Time) Scalability.
>
> **When to use:** On all projects; this approach is the most cost effective (resources and time) to ensure scalability.
>
> **How to use:**
>
> - Design for 20x capacity.
> - Implement for 3x capacity.
> - Deploy for ~1.5x capacity.
>
> **Why:** D-I-D provides a cost effective, JIT method of scaling your product.
>
> **Key takeaways:** Teams can save a lot of money and time by thinking of how to scale solutions early, implementing (coding) them a month or so before they are needed, and implementing them days before the customer rush or demand.

Our firm is focused on helping clients through their scalability needs, and as you might imagine customers often ask us "When should we invest in scalability?" The somewhat flippant answer is that you should invest (and deploy) the day before the solution is needed. If you could deploy scale improvements the day before you needed them, you would delay investments to be "just in time" and gain the benefits that Dell brought to the world with configure-to-order systems married with just in time manufacturing. In so doing you would maximize firm profits and shareholder wealth.

But let's face it—timing such an investment and deployment "just in time" is simply impossible, and even if possible it would incur a great deal of risk if you did not nail the date exactly. The next best thing to investing and deploying "the day before" is AKF Partners' *Design-Implement-Deploy* or *D-I-D* approach to thinking about scalability. These phases match the cognitive phases with which we are all familiar: starting to think about and designing a solution to a problem, building or coding a solution to that problem, and actually installing or deploying the solution to the problem. This approach does not argue for nor does it need a waterfall model. We argue that agile methodologies abide by such a process by the very definition of the need for human involvement. One cannot develop a solution to a problem of which they are not aware, and a solution cannot be manufactured or released if it is not developed. Regardless of the development methodology (agile, waterfall, hybrid, or whatever), everything we develop should be based on a set of architectural principles and standards that define and guide what we do.

Design

We start with the notion that discussing and designing something is significantly less expensive than actually implementing that design in code. Given this relatively low cost we can discuss and sketch out a design for how to scale our platform well in advance of our need. Whereas we clearly would not want to put 10x, 20x, or 100x more capacity than we would need in our production environment, the cost of discussing how to scale something to those dimensions is comparatively small. The focus then in the (D)esign phase of the D-I-D scale model is on scaling to between 20x and infinity. Our intellectual costs are high as we employ our "big thinkers" to think through the "big problems." Engineering and asset costs, however, are low as we aren't writing code or deploying costly systems. Scalability summits, a process in which groups of leaders and engineers gather to discuss scale limiting aspects of the product, are a good way to identify the areas necessary to scale within the design phase of the D-I-D process. Table 1.1 lists the parts of the D-I-D process.

Table 1.1   **D-I-D Process for Scale**

	Design	Implement	Deploy
Scale Objective	20x to Infinite	3x to 20x	1.5x to 3x
Intellectual Cost	High	Medium	Low to Medium
Engineering Cost	Low	High	Medium
Asset Cost	Low	Low to Medium	High to Very High
Total Cost	Low/Medium	Medium	Medium

Implement

As time moves on, and as our perceived need for future scale draws near, we move to (I)mplementing our designs within our software. We reduce our scope in terms of scale needs to something that's more realistic, such as 3x to 20x our current size. We use "size" here to identify that element of the system that is perceived to be the greatest bottleneck of scale and therefore in the greatest need of modification for scalability. There may be cases where the cost of scaling 100x (or greater) our current size is not different than the cost of scaling 20x, and if this is the case we might as well make those changes once rather than going in and making those changes multiple times. This might be the case if we are going to perform a modulus of our user base to distribute (or share) them across multiple (N) systems and databases. We might code a variable Cust_MOD that we can configure over time between 1 (today) and 1,000 (5 years from now). The engineering (or implementation) cost of such a change really doesn't vary with the size of N so we might as well make it. The cost of these types of changes are high in terms of engineering time, medium in terms of intellectual time (we already discussed the designs earlier in our lifecycle), and low in terms of assets as we don't need to deploy 100x our systems today if we intend to deploy a modulus of 1 or 2 in our first phase.

Deployment

The final phase of the D-I-D process is (D)eployment. Using our modulus example above, we want to deploy our systems in a just in time fashion; there's no reason to have idle assets sitting around diluting shareholder value. Maybe we put 1.5x of our peak capacity in production if we are a moderately high growth company and 5x our peak capacity in production if we are a hyper growth company. We often guide our clients to leverage the "cloud" for burst capacity so that we don't have 33% of our assets waiting around for a sudden increase in user activity. Asset costs are high in the deployment phase, and other costs range from low to medium. Total costs tend to be highest for this category as to deploy 100x of your necessary capacity relative to demand would kill many companies. Remember that scale is an elastic concept; it can both expand and contract, and our solutions should recognize both aspects of scale. Flexibility is therefore key as you may need to move capacity around as different systems within your solution expand and contract to customer demand.

Referring to Table 1.1, we can see that while each phase of the D-I-D process has varying intellectual, engineering, and asset costs, there is a clear progression of overall cost to the company. Designing and thinking about scale comes relatively cheaply and thus should happen frequently. Ideally these activities result in some sort of written documentation so that others can build upon it quickly should the need arise. Engineering (or developing) the architected or designed solutions can happen later and cost a bit more overall, but there is no need to actually implement them in production. We can roll the code and make small modifications as in our modulus example above without needing to purchase 100x the number of systems we have today. Finally the process lends itself nicely to purchasing equipment just ahead of our need, which might be a six-week lead time from a major equipment provider or having one of our systems administrators run down to the local server store in extreme emergencies.

Rule 3—Simplify the Solution 3 Times Over

Rule 3: What, When, How, and Why

What: Used when designing complex systems, this rule simplifies the scope, design, and implementation.

When to use: When designing complex systems or products where resources (engineering or computational) are limited.

How to use:

- Simplify scope using the Pareto Principle.
- Simplify design by thinking about cost effectiveness and scalability.
- Simplify implementation by leveraging the experience of others.

> **Why:** Focusing just on "not being complex" doesn't address the issues created in requirements or story and epoch development or the actual implementation.
>
> **Key takeaways:** Simplification needs to happen during every aspect of product development.

Whereas Rule 1 dealt with avoiding surpassing the "usable" requirements and eliminating complexity, this rule discusses taking another pass at simplifying everything from your perception of your needs through your actual design and implementation. Rule 1 is about fighting against the urge to make something overly complex, and Rule 3 is about attempting to further simplify the solution by the methods described herein. Sometimes we tell our clients to think of this rule as "asking the 3 how's." How do I simplify my scope, my design, and my implementation?

How Do I Simplify the Scope?

The answer to this question of simplification is to apply the Pareto Principle (also known as the 80–20 rule) frequently. What 80% of your benefit is achieved from 20% of the work? In our case, a direct application is to ask "what 80% of your revenue will be achieved by 20% of your features." Doing significantly less (20% of the work) and achieving significant benefits (80% of the value) frees up your team to perform other tasks. If you cut unnecessary features from your product, you can do 5x as much work, and your product would be significantly less complex! With 4/5ths fewer features, your system will no doubt have fewer dependencies between functions and as a result will be able to scale both more effectively and cost effectively. Moreover, the 80% of the time that is freed up can be used to both launch new product offerings as well as invest in thinking ahead to the future scalability needs of your product.

We're not alone in our thinking on how to reduce unnecessary features while keeping a majority of the benefit. The folks at 37signals are huge proponents of this approach, discussing the need and opportunity to prune work in both their book *Rework*[2] and in their blog post titled "You Can Always Do Less."[3] Indeed, the concept of the "minimum viable product" popularized by Eric Reis and evangelized by Marty Cagan is predicated on the notion of maximizing the "amount of validated learning about customers with the least effort."[4] This "agile" focused approach allows us to release simple, easily scalable products quickly. In so doing we get greater product throughput in our organizations (organizational scalability) and can spend additional time focusing on building the minimal product in a more scalable fashion. By simplifying our scope we have more computational power as we are doing less.

How Do I Simplify My Design?

With this new smaller scope, the job of simplifying our implementation just became easier. Simplifying design is closely related to the complexity aspect of overengineering. Complexity elimination is about cutting off unnecessary trips in a job, and simplification is about finding a shorter path. In Rule 1, we gave the example of only asking a database for that which you need; `select(*) from schema_name.table_name` became `select (column) from schema_name.table_name`. The approach of design simplification suggests that we first look to see if we already have the information being requested within a local shared resource like local memory. Complexity elimination is about doing less work, and design simplification is about doing that work faster and easier.

Imagine a case where we are looking to read some source data, perform a computation on intermediate tokens from this source data, and then bundle up these tokens. In many cases, each of these verbs might be broken into a series of services. In fact, this approach looks similar to that employed by the popular "map-reduce" algorithm. This approach isn't overly complex, so it doesn't violate Rule 1. But if we know that files to be read are small and we don't need to combine tokens across files, it might make sense to take the simple path of making this a simple monolithic application rather than decomposing it into services. Going back to our timecard example, if the goal is simply to compute hours for a single individual it makes sense to have multiple cloned monolithic applications reading a queue of timecards and performing the computations. Put simply, the step of design simplification asks us how to get the job done in an easy to understand, cost-effective, and scalable way.

How Do I Simplify My Implementation?

Finally, we get to the question of implementation. Consistent with Rule 2—the D-I-D Process for Scale, we define an implementation as the actual coding of a solution. This is where we get into questions such as whether it makes more sense to solve a problem with recursion or iteration. Should we define an array of a certain size, or be prepared to allocate memory dynamically as we need it? Do I make the solution, open-source the solution, or buy it? The answers to all these solutions have a consistent theme: "How can we leverage the experiences of others and existing solutions to simplify our implementation?"

Given that we can't be the best at building everything, we should first look to find widely adopted open source or third-party solutions to meet our needs. If those don't exist, we should look to see if someone within our own organization has developed a scalable solution to solve the problem. In the absence of a proprietary solution, we should again look externally to see if someone has described a scalable approach to solve the problem that we can legally copy or mimic. Only in the absence of finding one of these three things should we embark on attempting to solve the solution ourselves. The simplest implementation is almost always one that has already been implemented and proven scalable.

Rule 4—Reduce DNS Lookups

Rule 4: What, When, How, and Why

What: Reduce the number of DNS lookups from a user perspective.

When to use: On all Web pages where performance matters.

How to use: Minimize the number of DNS lookups required to download pages, but balance this with the browser's limitation for simultaneous connections.

Why: DNS lookups take a great deal of time, and large numbers of them can amount to a large portion of your user experience.

Key takeaways: Reduction of objects, tasks, computation, and so on is a great way of speeding up page load time, but division of labor must be considered as well.

As we've seen so far in this chapter, reducing is the name of the game for performance improvements and increased scalability. A lot of rules are focused on the architecture of the Software as a Service (SaaS) solution, but for this rule let's consider your customer's browser. If you use any of the browser level debugging tools such as Mozilla Firefox's plug-in Firebug,[5] you'll see some interesting results when you load a page from your application. One of the things you will most likely notice is that similarly sized objects on your page take different amounts of time to download. As you look closer you'll see some of these objects have an additional step at the beginning of their download. This additional step is the DNS lookup.

The Domain Name System (DNS) is one of the most important parts of the infrastructure of the Internet or any other network that utilizes the Internet Protocol Suite (TCP/IP). It allows the translation from domain name (www.akfpartners.com) to an IP address (184.72.236.173) and is often analogized to a phone book. DNS is maintained by a distributed database system, the nodes of which are the name servers. The top of the hierarchy consists of the root name servers. Each domain has at least one authoritative DNS server that publishes information about that domain.

This process of translating domains into IP addresses is made quicker by caching on many levels, including the browser, computer operating system, Internet service provider, and so on. However, in our world where pages can have hundreds or thousands of objects, many from different domains, small milliseconds of time can add up to something noticeable to the customer.

Before we go any deeper into our discussion of reducing the DNS lookups we need to understand at a high level how most browsers download pages. This isn't meant to be an in-depth study of browsers, but understanding the basics will help you optimize your application's performance and scalability. Browsers take advantage of the fact that almost all Web pages are comprised of many different objects (images, JavaScript files, css files, and so on) by having the ability to download multiple objects through simultaneous connections. Browsers limit the maximum number of simultaneous persistent connections per server or proxy. According to the HTTP/1.1 RFC[6] this maximum should be set to 2; however, many browsers now ignore this RFC and have maximums of 6 or more. We'll talk about how to optimize your page download time based on this functionality in the next rule. For now let's focus on our Web page broken up into many objects and able to be downloaded through multiple connections.

Every distinct domain that serves one or more objects for a Web page requires a DNS lookup either from cache or out to a DNS name server. For example, let's assume we have a simple Web page that has four objects: 1) the HTML page itself that contains text and directives for other objects, 2) a CSS file for the layout, 3) a JavaScript file for a menu item, and 4) a JPG image. The HTML comes from our domain (akfpartners.com), but the CSS and JPG are served from a subdomain (static.akf-partners.com), and the JavaScript we've linked to from Google (ajax.googleapis.com). In this scenario our browser first receives the request to go to page www.akfpartners.com, which requires a DNS lookup of the akfpartners.com domain. Once the HTML is downloaded the browser parses it and finds that it needs to download the CSS and JPG both from static.akfpart-ners.com, which requires another DNS lookup. Finally, the pars-ing reveals the need for an external JavaScript file from yet another domain. Depending on the freshness of DNS cache in our browser, operating system, and so on, this lookup can take essentially no time up to hundreds of milliseconds. Figure 1.1 shows a graphical representation of this.

As a general rule, the fewer DNS lookups on your pages the better your page download performance will be. There is a downside to combining all your objects into a single domain, and we've hinted at the reason in the previous discussion about maximum simultaneous connects. We explore this topic in more detail in the next rule.

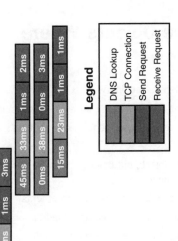

Figure 1.1   Object download time

Rule 5—Reduce Objects Where Possible

Rule 5: What, When, How, and Why

What: Reduce the number of objects on a page where possible.

When to use: On all web pages where performance matters.

How to use:

- Reduce or combine objects but balance this with maximizing simultaneous connections.
- Test changes to ensure performance improvements.

Why: The number of objects impacts page download times.

Key takeaways: The balance between objects and methods that serve them is a science that requires constant measurement and adjustment; it's a balance between customer usability, usefulness, and performance.

Web pages consist of many different objects (HTML, CSS, images, JavaScript, and so on), which allows our browsers to download them somewhat independently and often in parallel. One of the easiest ways to improve Web page performance and thus increase your scalability (fewer objects to serve per page means your servers can serve more pages) is to reduce the number of objects on a page. The biggest offenders on most pages are graphical objects such as pictures and images. As an example let's take a look at Google's search page (www.google.com), which by their own admission is minimalist in nature.[7] At the time of writing Google had five objects on the search page: the HTML, two images, and two JavaScript files. In my very unscientific experiment the search page loaded in about 300 milliseconds. Compare this to a client that we were working with in the online magazine industry, whose home page had more than 200 objects, 145 of which were images and took on average more than 11 seconds to load. What this client didn't realize was that slow page performance was causing them to lose valuable readers. Google published a white paper in 2009 claiming that tests showed an increase in search latency of 400 milliseconds reduced their daily searches by almost 0.6%.[8]

Reducing the number of objects on the page is a great way to improve performance and scalability, but before you rush off to remove all your images there are a few other things to consider. First is obviously the important information that you are trying to convey to your customers. With no images your page will look like the 1992 W3 Project page, which claimed to be the first Web page.[9] Since you need images and JavaScript and CSS files, your second consideration might be to combine all similar objects into a single file. This is not a bad idea, and in fact there are techniques such as CSS image sprites for this exact purpose. An image sprite is a combination of small images into one larger image that can be manipulated with CSS to display any single individual image. The benefit of this is that the number of images requested is significantly reduced. Back to our discussion on the Google search page, one of the two images on the search page is a sprite that consists of about two dozen smaller images that can be individually displayed or not.[10]

So far we've covered that reducing the number of objects on a page will improve performance and scalability, but this must be balanced with the need for modern looking pages thus requiring images, CSS, and JavaScript. Next we covered how these can be combined into a single object to reduce the number of distinct requests that must be made by the browser to render the page. Yet another balance to be made is that combining everything into a single object doesn't make use of the maximum number of simultaneous persistent connections per server that we discussed previously in Rule 3. As a recap this is the browser's capability to download multiple objects simultaneously from a single domain. If everything is in one object, having the capability to download two or more simultaneous objects doesn't help. Now we need to think about breaking these objects back up into a number of smaller ones that can be downloaded simultaneously. One final variable to add to the equation is that part above about simultaneous persistent connections "per server, which will bring us full circle to our DNS discussion noted in Rule 4.

The simultaneous connection feature of a browser is a limit ascribed to each domain that is serving the objects. If all objects on your page come from a single domain (www.akfpartners. com), then whatever the browser has set as the maximum number of connections is the most objects that can be down-loaded simultaneously. As mentioned previously, this maximum is suggested to be set at 2, but many browsers by default have increased this to 6 or more. Therefore, you want your content (images, CSS, JavaScript, and so on) divided into enough objects to take advantage of this feature in most browsers. One tech-nique to really take advantage of this browser feature is to serve different objects from different subdomains (for example, static1.akfpartners.com, static2.akfpartners.com, and so on). The browser considers each of these different domains and allows for each to have the maximum connects concurrently. The client that we talked about earlier who was in the online magazine industry and had an 11-second page load time used this tech-nique across seven subdomains and was able to reduce the average load time to less than 5 seconds.

Unfortunately there is not an absolute answer about ideal size of objects or how many subdomains you should consider. The key to improving performance and scalability is testing your pages. There is a balance between necessary content and func-tionality, object size, rendering time, total download time, domains, and so on. If you have 100 images on a page, each 50KB, combining them into a single sprite is probably not a great idea because the page will not be able to display any images until the entire 4.9MB object downloads. The same con-cept goes for JavaScript. If you combine all your .js files into one, your page cannot use any of the JavaScript functions until the entire file is downloaded. The way to know for sure which is the best alternative is to test your pages on a variety of browsers with a variety of ISP connection speeds.

In summary, the fewer the number of objects on a page the better for performance, but this must be balanced with many other factors. Included in these factors are the amount of con-tent that must be displayed, how many objects can be combined, how to maximize the use of simultaneous connections by adding domains, the total page weight and whether penalization can help, and so on. While this rule touches on many Web site per-formance improvement techniques the real focus is how to improve performance and thus increase the scalability of your site through the reduction of objects on the page. Many other techniques for optimizing performance should be considered, including loading CSS at the top of the page and JavaScript files at the bottom, minifying files, and making use of caches, lazy loading, and so on.

Rule 6—Use Homogenous Networks

Rule 6: What, When, How, and Why

What: Don't mix the vendor networking gear.

When to use: When designing or expanding your network.

How to use:

- Do not mix different vendors' networking gear (switches and routers).
- Buy best of breed for other networking gear (firewalls, load balancers, and so on).

Why: Intermittent interoperability and availability issues simply aren't worth the potential cost savings.

Key takeaways: Heterogeneous networking gear tends to cause availability and scalability problems. Choose a single provider.

We are technology agnostic, meaning that we believe almost any technology can be made to scale when architected and deployed correctly. This agnosticism ranges from programming language preference to database vendors to hardware. The one caveat to this is with network gear such as routers and switches. Almost all the vendors claim that they implement standard protocols (for example, Internet Control Message Protocol RFC792,[11] Routing Information Protocol RFC1058,[12] Border Gateway Protocol RFC4271[13]) that allow for devices from different vendors to communicate, but many also implement proprietary protocols such as Cisco's Enhanced Interior Gateway Routing Protocol (EIGRP). What we've found in our own practice, as well as with many of our customers, is that each vendor's interpretation of how to implement a standard is often different. As an analogy, if you've ever developed the user interface for a Web page and tested it in a couple different browsers such as Internet

Explorer, Firefox, and Chrome, you've seen firsthand how different implementations of standards can be. Now, imagine that going on inside your network. Mixing Vendor A's network devices with Vendor B's network devices is asking for trouble.

This is not to say that we prefer one vendor over another—we don't. As long as they are a "reference-able" standard utilized by customers larger than you, in terms of network traffic volume, we don't have a preference. This rule does not apply to networking gear such as hubs, load balancers, and firewalls. The network devices that we care about in terms of homogeneity are the ones that must communicate to route communication. For all the other network devices that may or may not be included in your network such as intrusion detection systems (IDS), firewalls, load balancers, and distributed denial of service (DDOS) protection appliances, we recommend best of breed choices. For these devices choose the vendor that best serves your needs in terms of features, reliability, cost, and service.

Summary

This chapter was about making things simpler. Guarding against complexity (aka overengineering—Rule 1) and simplifying every step of your product from your initial requirements or stories through the final implementation (Rule 3) gives us products that are easy to understand from an engineering perspective and therefore easy to scale. By thinking about scale early (Rule 2) even if we don't implement it, we can have solutions ready on demand for our business. Rules 4 and 5 teach us to reduce the work we force browsers to do by reducing the number of objects and DNS lookups we must make to download those objects. Rule 6 teaches us to keep our networks simple and homogenous to decrease the chances of scale and availability problems associated with mixed networking gear.

Endnotes

1. Wikipedia, "Overengineering," http://en.wikipedia.org/wiki/
    Overengineering.
2. Jason Fried and David Heinemeier Hansson, *Rework* (New York:
    Crown Business, 2010).
3. 37Signals, "You Can Always Do Less," Signal vs. Noise blog,
    January 14, 2010, http://37signals.com/svn/posts/2106-you-can-
    always-do-less.
4. Wikipedia, "Minimum Viable Product," http://en.wikipedia.org/wiki/
    Minimum_viable_product.
5. To get or install Firebug, go to http://getfirebug.com/.
6. R. Fielding, J. Gettys, J. Mogul, H. Frystyk, L. Masinter, P. Leach, and
    T. Berners-Lee, Network Working Group Request for Comments
    2616, "Hypertext Transfer Protocol—HTTP/1.1," June 1999,
    www.ietf.org/rfc/rfc2616.txt.
7. The Official Google Blog, "A Spring Metamorphosis—Google's New
    Look," May 5, 2010, http://googleblog.blogspot.com/2010/05/
    spring-metamorphosis-googles-new-look.html.
8. Jake Brutlag, "Speed Matters for Google Web Search," Google, Inc.,
    June 2009, http://code.google.com/speed/files/delayexp.pdf.
9. World Wide Web, www.w3.org/History/19921103-hypertext/
    hypertext/WWW/TheProject.html.
10. Google.com, www.google.com/images/srpr/nav_logo14.png.
11. J. Postel, Network Working Group Request for Comments 792,
    "Internet Control Message Protocol," September 1981, http://tools.
    ietf.org/html/rfc792.
12. C. Hedrick, Network Working Group Request for Comments 1058,
    "Routing Information Protocol," June 1988, http://tools.ietf.org/
    html/rfc1058.
13. Y. Rekhter, T. Li, and S. Hares, eds., Network Working Group Request
    for Comments 4271, "A Border Gateway Protocol 4 (BGP-4)," January
    2006, http://tools.ietf.org/html/rfc4271.

2

Distribute Your Work

When you hear the word *distribute* you might immediately think of grid computing—the concept of dividing tasks into small chunks of work that can be farmed out to two or more computers, each of which performs a piece of the task necessary for the final answer. If you're interested in that topic, you should see Chapters 28 and 30 of *The Art of Scalability*. In this chapter we discuss how you can distribute your data and application services across multiple systems to ensure you have the ability to scale to meet your customer's demands.

The concept of distributing work can be analogized to painting a picket fence. Let's say you and your four friends want to play baseball but you've been tasked with painting the fence before you can play. If you have 25 pickets (vertical posts) that you need to paint white and each picket takes 1 minute to paint, you could complete this task in 25 minutes (give or take for cleanup and other miscellaneous tasks). Alternatively, your four buddies could each pick up a paintbrush, instead of lying around asking you to hurry up, and help paint. With five people painting 1 picket each per minute, you can be done and on your way to play baseball in a matter of just 5 minutes (25 pickets / 5 people × 1 picket per person per minute). The lesson learned is the more you can divide up the work the greater throughput (work/time) that you can achieve resulting in greater scalability.

This chapter discusses scaling databases and services through cloning and replication, separating functionality or services, and splitting similar data sets across storage and application systems.

Utilizing these three approaches, you will be able to scale nearly any system or database to a level that approaches infinite scalability. We use the word *approaches* here as a bit of a hedge, but in our experience across more than a hundred companies and thousands of databases and systems these techniques have yet to fail. To help visualize these three approaches to scale we employ the AKF Scale Cube, a diagram we developed to represent these methods of scaling systems. Figure 2.1 shows the AKF Scale Cube, which is named after our partnership, AKF Partners.

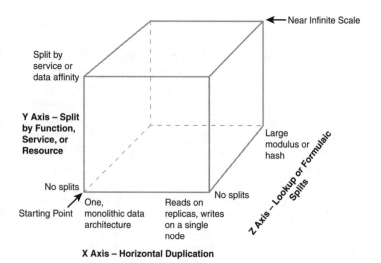

Figure 2.1   AKF Scale Cube

At the heart of the AKF Scale Cube are three simple axes, each with an associated rule for scalability. The cube is a great way to represent the path from minimal scale (lower-left front of the cube) to near infinite scalability (upper-right back corner of the cube). Sometimes, it's easier to see these three axes without the confined space of the cube. Figure 2.2 shows these three axes along with their associated rules. We cover each of these three rules in this chapter.

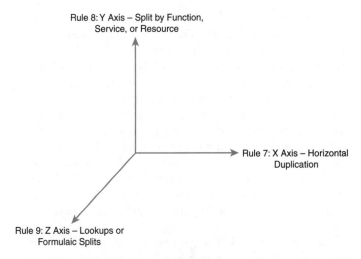

Figure 2.2   Three axes of scale

Rule 7—Design to Clone Things (X Axis)

Rule 7: What, When, How, and Why

What: Typically called horizontal scale, this is the duplication of services or databases to spread transaction load.

When to use:

- Databases with a very high read to write ratio (5:1 or greater—the higher the better).
- Any system where transaction growth exceeds data growth.

How to use:

- Simply clone services and implement a load balancer.
- For databases, ensure the accessing code understands the difference between a read and a write.

Why: Allows for fast scale of transactions at the cost of duplicated data and functionality.

Key takeaways: X axis splits are fast to implement and can allow for transaction, but not data scalability.

The hardest part of a system to scale is almost always the database or persistent storage tier. The beginning of this problem can be traced back to Edgar F. Codd's 1970 paper "A Relational Model of Data for Large Shared Data Banks"[1] which is credited with introducing the concept of the Relational Database Management System (RDBMS). Today's most popular RDBMSs, such as Oracle, MySQL, and SQL Server, just as the name implies, allow for relations between data elements. These relationships can exist within or between tables. The tables of most On Line Transactional Processing (OLTP) systems are normalized to third normal form,[2] where all records of a table have the same fields, nonkey fields cannot be described by only one of the keys in a composite key, and all nonkey fields must be described by the key. Within the table each piece of data is related to other pieces of data in that table. Between tables there are often relationships, known as foreign keys. Most applications depend on the database to support and enforce these relationships because of its ACID properties (see Table 2.1). Requiring the database to maintain and enforce these relationships makes it difficult to split the database without significant engineering effort.

Table 2.1   ACID Properties of Databases

Property	Description
Atomicity	All of the operations in the transaction will complete, or none will.
Consistency	The database will be in a consistent state when the transaction begins and ends.
Isolation	The transaction will behave as if it is the only operation being performed upon the database.
Durability	Upon completion of the transaction, the operation will not be reversed.

One technique for scaling databases is to take advantage of the fact that most applications and databases perform significantly more reads than writes. A client of ours that handles booking reservations for customers has on average 400 searches for a single booking. Each booking is a write and each search a read, resulting in a 400:1 read to write ratio. This type of system can be easily scaled by creating read-only copies (or replicas) of the data

There are a couple ways that you can distribute the read-copy of your data depending on the time sensitivity of the data. Time sensitivity is how fresh or completely correct the read-copy has to be relative to the write copy. Before you scream out that the data has to be instantly, real time, in sync, and completely correct across the entire system, take a breath and appreciate the costs of such a system. While perfectly in sync data is ideal, it costs…a lot. Furthermore, it doesn't always give you the return that you might expect or desire for that cost.

Let's go back to our client with the reservation system that has 400 reads for every write. They're handling reservations for customers so you would think the data they display to customers would have to be completely in sync. For starters you'd be keeping 400 sets of data in sync for the 1 piece of data that the customer wants to reserve. Second, just because the data is out of sync with the primary transactional database by 3 or 30 or 90 seconds doesn't mean that it isn't correct, just that there is a chance that it isn't correct. This client probably has 100,000 pieces of data in their system at any one time and books 10% of those each day. If those bookings are evenly distributed across the course of a day they are booking one reservation just about every second (0.86 sec). All things being equal, the chance of a customer wanting a particular booking that is already taken by another customer (assuming a 90 second sync of data) is 0.104%. Of course even at 0.1% some customers will select a booking that is already taken, which might not be ideal but can be handled in the application by doing a final check before allowing the booking to be placed in their cart. Certainly every application's data needs are going to be different, but from this discussion hopefully you will get a sense of how you can push back on the idea that all data has to be kept in sync in real time.

Now that we've covered the time sensitivity, let's start discussing the ways to distribute the data. One way is to use a caching tier in front of the database. An object cache can be used to read from instead of going back to the application for each query. Only when the data has been marked expired would the application have to query the primary transactional database to retrieve the data and refresh the cache. Given the availability of numerous excellent, open source key-value stores that can be used as object caches, this is a highly recommended first step.

The next step beyond an object cache between the application tier and the database tier, is replicating the database. Most major relational database systems allow for some type of replication "out of the box." MySQL implements replication through the *master-slave* concept—the master database being the primary transactional database that gets written to and the slave databases are read-only copies of the master databases. The master database keeps track of updates, inserts, deletes, and so on in a binary log. Each slave requests the binary log from the master and replays these commands on its database. While this is asynchronous, the latency between data being updated in the master and then in the slave can be very low. Often this implementation consists of several slave databases or read replicas that are configured behind a load balancer. The application makes a read request to the load balancer, which passes the request in either a round robin or least connections manner to a read replica.

We call this type of split an X axis split, and it is represented on the AKF Scale Cube in Figure 2.1 as the X axis – Horizontal Duplication. An example that many developers familiar with hosting Web applications will recognize is on the Web or application tier of a system, running multiple servers behind a load balancer all with the same code. A request comes in to the load balancer that distributes it to any one of the many Web or application servers to fulfill. The great thing about this distributed model on the application tier is that you can put dozens, hundreds, or even thousands of servers behind load balancers all running the same code and handling similar requests.

The X axis can be applied to more than just the database. Web servers and application servers typically can be easily cloned. This cloning allows the distribution of transactions across systems evenly for horizontal scale. This cloning of application or Web services tends to be relatively easy to perform, and allows us to scale the number of transactions processed. Unfortunately, it doesn't really help us when trying to scale the data we must manipulate to perform these transactions. In memory, caching of

data unique to several customers or unique to disparate functions
might create a bottleneck that keeps us from scaling these services without significant impact to customer response time. To solve
these memory constraints we'll look to the Y and Z axes of our
scale cube.

Rule 8—Design to Split Different Things (Y Axis)

Rule 8: What, When, How, and Why

What: Sometimes referred to as scale through services or
resources, this rule focuses on scaling data sets, transactions,
and engineering teams.

When to use:

- Very large data sets where relations between data are not
  necessary.
- Large, complex systems where scaling engineering
  resources requires specialization.

How to use:

- Split up actions by using verbs or resources by using
  nouns or use a mix.
- Split both the services and the data along the lines
  defined by the verb/noun approach.

Why: Allows for efficient scaling of not only transactions, but very
large data sets associated with those transactions.

Key takeaways: Y axis or data/service-oriented splits, allow for
efficient scaling of transactions, large data sets, and can help
with fault isolation.

When you put aside the religious debate around the concepts of
services (SOA) and resources (ROA) oriented architectures and
look deep into their underlying premises, they have at least one
thing in common. Both concepts force architects and engineers
to think in terms of separation of responsibilities within their
architectures. At a high and simple level, they do this through the
concepts of verbs (services) and nouns (resources). Rule 8, and
our second axis of scale, takes the same approach. Put simply,

Rule 8 is about scaling through the separation of distinct and different functions and data within your site. The simple approach to Rule 8 tells us to split up our product by either nouns or verbs or a combination of both nouns and verbs.

Let's split up our site using the verb approach first. If our site is a relatively simple ecommerce site, we might break our site into the necessary verbs of signup, login, search, browse, view, add-to-cart, and purchase/buy. The data necessary to perform any one of these transactions can vary significantly from the data necessary for the other transactions. For instance, while signup and login might be argued to need the same data, they have some data that is unique and distinct. Signup, for instance, probably needs to be capable of checking whether a user's preferred ID has been chosen by someone else in the past, while login might not need to have a complete understanding of every other user's ID. Signup likely needs to write a fair amount of data to some permanent data store, while login is likely a read-intensive application to validate a user's credentials. Signup may require that the user store a fair amount of personally identifiable information including credit card numbers, while login does not likely need access to all of this information at the time that a user would like to establish a login.

The differences and resulting opportunities for this method of scale become even more apparent when we analyze obviously distinct functions as is the case between search and login. In the case of login we are mostly concerned with validating the user's credentials and potentially establishing some notion of session (we've chosen the word *session* rather than *state* for a reason we explore in Rule 40). Login is concerned about the user and as a result needs to cache and interact with data about that user. Search, on the other hand, is concerned about the hunt for an item and is most concerned about user intent (vis-à-vis a search string, query, or search terms typically typed into a search box) and the items that we have in stock within our catalog of items. Separating these sets of data allows us to cache more of them within the confines of memory available on our system and process transactions faster as a result of higher cache hit ratios. Separating this data within our backend persistence systems (such as a database) allows us to dedicate more "in memory" space within those systems and respond faster to the clients (application servers) making requests. Both systems respond faster as a result of better utilization of system resources. Clearly we can now scale these systems more easily and with less memory constraints. Moreover, the Y axis adds transaction scalability by splitting up transactions in the same fashion as Rule 7, the X axis of scale.

Hold on! What if we want to merge information about the user and our products such as in the case of recommending products? Note that we have just added another verb—*recommend*. This gives us another opportunity to perform a split of our data and our transactions. We might add a recommendation service that asynchronously evaluates past user purchase behavior with users of similar purchase behaviors. This in turn may populate data in either the login function or the search function for display to the user when he or she interacts with the system. Or it can be a separate synchronous call made from the user's browser to be displayed in an area dedicated to the result of the recommend call.

Now how about using nouns to split items? Again, using our ecommerce example we might identify certain resources upon which we will ultimately take actions (rather than the verbs that represent the actions we take). We may decide that our ecommerce site is made up of a product catalog, product inventory, user account information, marketing information, and so on. Using our noun approach, we may decide to split up our data by these categories and then define a set of high-level primitives such as create, read, update, and delete actions on these primitives.

While Y axis splits are most useful in scaling data sets, they are also useful in scaling code bases. Because services or resources are now split, the actions we perform and the code necessary to perform them are split up as well. This means that very large engineering teams developing complex systems can become experts in subsets of those systems and don't need to worry about or become experts on every other part of the system. And of course because we have split up our services, we can also scale transactions fairly easily.

Rule 9—Design to Split Similar Things (Z Axis)

Rule 9: What, When, How, and Why

What: This is very often a split by some unique aspect of the customer such as customer ID, name, geography, and so on.

When to use: Very large, similar data sets such as large and rapidly growing customer bases.

How to use: Identify something you know about the customer, such as customer ID, last name, geography, or device and split or partition both data and services based on that attribute.

Why: Rapid customer growth exceeds other forms of data growth or you have the need to perform fault isolation between certain customer groups as you scale.

Key takeaways: Z axis splits are effective at helping you to scale customer bases but can also be applied to other very large data sets that can't be pulled apart using the Y axis methodology.

Often referred to as *sharding* and *podding*, Rule 9 is about taking one data set or service and partitioning it into several pieces. These pieces are often equal sized but may be of different sizes if there is value in having several unequal sized chunks or shards. One reason to have unequal sized shards is to enable application rollouts that limit your risk by affecting first a small customer segment, and then increasingly large segments of customers as you feel you have identified and resolved major problems.

Often sharding is accomplished by separating something we know about the requestor or customer. Let's say that we are a timecard and attendance tracking software as a service provider. We are responsible for tracking the time and attendance for employees for each of our clients who are in turn enterprise class customers with more than 1,000 employees each. We might determine that we can easily partition or shard our solution by company, meaning that each company could have its own dedicated Web, application, and database servers. Given that we also want to leverage the cost efficiencies enabled by multitenancy, we also want to have multiple small companies exist within a single shard. Really big companies with many employees might get dedicated hardware, while smaller companies with fewer employees cohabit within a larger number of shards. We have leveraged the fact that there is a relationship between employees and companies to create scalable partitions of systems that allow us to employ smaller, cost-effective hardware and scale horizontally (we discuss horizontal scale further in Rule 10).

Maybe we are a provider of advertising services for mobile phones. In this case, we very likely know something about the end user's device and carrier. Both of these create compelling characteristics by which we can partition our data. If we are an ecommerce player, we might split users by their geography to make more efficient use of our available inventory in distribution centers. Or maybe we create partitions of data that allow us to evenly distribute users based on the recency, frequency, and monetization of their purchases. Or, if all else fails, maybe we just use some modulus or hash of a user identification (userid) number that we've assigned the user at signup.

Why would we ever decide to partition similar things? For hyper growth companies, the answer is easy. The speed with which we can answer any request is at least partially determined by the cache hit ratio of near and distant caches. This speed in turn indicates how many transactions we can process on any given system, which in turn determines how many systems we need to process a number of requests. In the extreme case, without partitioning of data, our transactions might become agonizingly slow as we attempt to traverse huge amounts of monolithic data to come to a single answer for a single user. Where speed is paramount and the data to answer any request is large, designing to split different things (Rule 8) and similar things (Rule 9) become necessities.

Splitting similar things obviously isn't just limited to customers, but customers are the most often and easiest implementation of Rule 9 within our consulting practice. Sometimes we recommend splitting product catalogs for instance. But when we split diverse catalogs into items such as lawn chairs and diapers, we often categorize these as splits of different things. We've also helped clients shard their systems by splitting along a modulus or hash of a transaction ID. In these cases, we really don't know anything about the requestor, but we do have a monotonically increasing number upon which we can act. These types of splits can be performed on systems that log transactions for future reference as in a system designed to retain errors for future evaluation.

Summary

We maintain that three simple rules can help you scale nearly everything. There are undoubtedly more ways to scale systems and platforms, but armed with these three rules, few if any scale related problems will stand in your way:

- **Scale by cloning**—Cloning or duplicating data and services allows you to scale transactions easily.

- **Scale by splitting different things**—Use nouns or verbs to identify data and services to separate. If done properly, both transactions and data sets can be scaled efficiently.

- **Scale by splitting similar things**—Typically these are customer data sets. Set customers up into unique and separated shards or swimlanes (see Chapter 9, "Design for Fault Tolerance and Graceful Failure," for *swimlane* definition) to enable transaction and data scaling.

Endnotes

1. Edgar F. Codd, "A Relational Model of Data for Large Shared Data Banks," 1970, www.eecs.umich.edu/~klefevre/eecs584/Papers/codd_1970.pdf.
2. Wikipedia, "Third normal form," http://en.wikipedia.org/wiki/Third_normal_form.

3

Design to Scale Out Horizontally

Within our practice, we often tell clients that "Scaling up is failing up." What does that mean? In our minds, it's pretty clear: We believe that within hyper growth environments it is critical that companies plan to scale in a horizontal fashion through the segmentation of workloads. The practice or implementation of that segmentation often looks like one of the approaches we described in Chapter 2, "Distribute Your Work." When hyper growth companies do not scale out, their only option is to buy bigger and faster systems. When they hit the limitation of the fastest and biggest system provided by the most costly provider of the system in question they are in big trouble. Ultimately, this is what hurt eBay in 1999, and we still see it more than a decade later in our business and with our clients today. The constraints and problems with scaling up aren't only a physical issue. Often they are caused by a logical contention that bigger and faster hardware simply can't solve. This chapter discusses the thoughts behind why you should design your systems to scale horizontally, or *out*, rather than *up*.

Rule 10: Design Your Solution to Scale Out—Not Just Up

> ### Rule 10: What, When, How, and Why
>
> **What**: *Scaling out* is the duplication of services or databases to spread transaction load and is the alternative to buying larger hardware, known as *scaling up*.
>
> **When to use:** Any system, service, or database expected to grow rapidly.
>
> **How to use:** Use the AKF Scale Cube to determine the correct split for your environment. Usually the horizontal split (cloning) is the easiest.
>
> **Why**: Allows for fast scale of transactions at the cost of duplicated data and functionality.
>
> **Key takeaways:** Plan for success and design your systems to scale out. Don't get caught in the trap of expecting to scale up only to find out that you've run out of faster and larger systems to purchase.

What do you do when faced with a rapid growth of customers and transactions on your systems and you haven't built them to scale to multiple servers? Ideally you'd investigate your options and decide you could either buy a larger server or spend engineering time to enable the software to run on multiple servers. Having the ability to run your application or database on multiple servers is *scaling out*. Continuing to run your systems on larger hardware is *scaling up*. In your analysis, you might come to the decision through an ROI calculation that it is cheaper to buy the next larger server rather than spend the engineering resources required to change the application. While we would applaud the analytical approach to this decision, for very high-growth companies and products it's probably flawed. The reason is that it likely doesn't take into account the long-term costs. Moving from a machine with two 64-bit dual-core processors to one with four processors will likely cost proportionally exactly what you get in improved computational resources (~2x). The fallacy comes in as we continue to purchase larger servers with more processors. This curve of cost to computational processing is a power law in which the cost begins to increase disproportionally to the increase in processing power provided by larger servers (see Rule 11). Assuming that your company continues to succeed and grow, you will continue to travel up the curve in costs for bigger systems. While you may budget for technology refreshes over time, you will be forced to purchase systems at an incredibly high price point relative to the cheaper systems you could purchase if you had built to scale horizontally. Overall, your total capital expenditures increase significantly. Of course the costs to solve the problem with engineering resources will also likely increase due to the increased size of the code base and complexity of the system, but this cost should be linear. Thus your analysis in the beginning should have resulted in a decision to spend the time up front changing the code to scale out.

Using an online pricing and configuration utility from one of the large server vendors, the graph in Figure 3.1 shows the cost of seven servers each configured as closely as possible to one another (RAM, disk, and so on) except for the increasing number of processors and cores per processor. Admittedly the computational resource from two dual-core processors is not exactly equivalent to a single quad-core, but for this cost comparison it is close enough. Notice the exponential trend line that fits the data points.

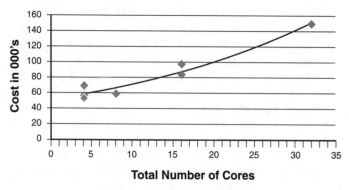

Figure 3.1   Cost per core

In our experience with more than a hundred clients, this type of analysis almost always results in the decision to modify the code or database to scale out instead of up. That's why it's an AKF Partners' belief that scaling up is failing up. Eventually you will get to a point that either the cost becomes uneconomical or there is no bigger hardware made. For example, we had a client who did have some ability to split their customers onto different systems but continued to scale up with their database hardware. They eventually topped out with six of the largest servers made by their preferred hardware vendor. Each of these systems cost more than $3 million, totaling nearly $20 million in hardware cost. Struggling to continue to scale as their customer demand increased, they undertook a project to horizontally scale their databases. They were able to replace each of those large servers with four much smaller servers costing $350,000 each. In the end they not only succeeded in continuing to scale for their customers but realized a savings of almost $10 million. The company continued to use the old systems until they ultimately failed with age and could be replaced with newer, smaller systems at lower cost.

Most applications are either built from the start to allow them to be run on multiple servers or they can be easily modified to accommodate this. For most SaaS applications this is as simple as replicating the code onto multiple application servers and putting them behind a load balancer. The application servers need not know about each other, but each request gets handled by whichever server gets sent the request from the load balancer. If the application has to keep track of state (see Chapter 10, "Avoid or Distribute State," for why you will want to eliminate this), a possible solution is to allow session cookies from the load balancer to maintain affinity between a customer's browser and a particular application server. Once the customer has made the initial request, whichever server was tasked with responding to that request will continue to handle that customer until the session has ended.

For a database to scale out often requires more planning and engineering work, but as we explained in the beginning this is almost always effort well spent. In Chapter 2, we covered three ways in which you can scale an application or database. These are identified on the AKF Scale Cube as X, Y, or Z axis corresponding to replicating (cloning), splitting different things (services), and splitting similar things (customers).

"But wait!" you cry. "Intel's co-founder Gordon Moore predicted in 1965 that the number of transistors that can be placed on an integrated circuit will double every two years." That's true. Moore's Law has amazingly held true for nearly 50 years now. The problem with this is that this "law" cannot hold true forever, as Gordon Moore admitted in a 2005 interview.[1] Additionally, if you are a true hyper growth company you are growing faster than just doubling customers or transactions every two years. You might be doubling every quarter. Relying on Moore's Law to scale your system, whether it's your application or database, is likely to lead to failure.

Rule 11—Use Commodity Systems (Goldfish Not Thoroughbreds)

> ### Rule 11: What, When, How, and Why
>
> **What:** Use small, inexpensive systems where possible.
>
> **When to use:** Use this approach in your production environment when going through hyper growth.
>
> **How to use:** Stay away from very large systems in your production environment.
>
> **Why:** Allows for fast, cost-effective growth.
>
> **Key takeaways:** Build your systems to be capable of relying on commodity hardware and don't get caught in the trap of using high-margin, high-end servers.

Hyper growth can be a lonely place. There's so much to learn and so little time to do that learning. But rest assured, if you follow our advice, you'll have lots of friends—lots of friends that draw power, create heat, push air, and do useful money making tasks—computers. And in our world, the world of hyper growth, we believe that a lot of little low-cost "goldfish" are better than a few big high-cost "thoroughbreds."

One of my favorite lines from an undergraduate calculus book is "It should be intuitively obvious to the casual observer that <insert some totally nonobvious statement here>". This particular statement left a mark on me, primarily because what was being discussed was neither intuitive nor obvious to me at the time. It might not seem obvious that having more of something, like many more "smaller" computers, is a better solution than having fewer, larger systems. In fact, more computers probably means more power, more space, and more cooling. The reason more and smaller is often better than less and bigger is twofold and described later in this chapter.

Your equipment provider is incented to sell you into his or her highest margin products. Make no mistake about it, they are talking to you to make money, and they make the most money when they sell you the equipment that has the highest or fattest margin for them. That equipment happens to be the systems that have the largest number of processors. Why is this so? Many companies rely on faster, bigger hardware to do their necessary workloads and are simply unwilling to invest in scaling their own infrastructure. As such, the equipment manufacturers can hold these companies hostage with higher prices and achieve higher margins. But there is an interesting conundrum within this approach as these faster, bigger machines aren't really capable of doing more work compared to an equivalent number of processors in smaller systems. On a per-CPU basis, there is an inefficiency that simply hasn't been solved for in these large machines. As you add CPUs, each CPU does slightly less work than it would in a single CPU system (regardless of cores). There are many reasons for this, including the inefficiency of scheduling algorithms for multiple processors, conflicts with memory bus access speeds, structural hazards, data hazards, and so on.

Think about what we just said carefully. You are paying more on a CPU basis, but actually doing less per CPU. You are getting nailed twice!

When confronted with the previous information, your providers will likely go through the relatively common first phase of denial. The wise ones will quickly move on and indicate that your total cost of ownership will go down as the larger units draw less aggregate power than the smaller units. In fact, they might say, you can work with one of their partners to partition (or *virtualize*) the systems to get the benefit of small systems and lower power drain. This brings us to our second point: We must do some math.

It might, in fact, be the case that the larger system will draw less power and save you money. As power costs increase and system costs decrease, there is no doubt that there is a "right size" system for you that maximizes power, system cost, and computing power. But your vendors aren't the best source of information for this. You should do the math on your own. It is highly unlikely that you should purchase the largest system available as that math nearly never works. To figure out what to do with the vendors' arguments, let's break them down into their component parts.

The math is easy. Look at power cost and unit power consumption as compared to an independent third-party benchmark on system utilization. We can find the right system for us that still fits the commodity range (in other words hasn't been marked up by the vendor as a high-end system) and maximizes the intersection of computing power with minimal power and space requirements. Total cost of ownership, in nearly all cases and when considering all costs, typically goes down.

On the topic of virtualization, remember that no software comes for free. There are many reasons to *virtualize* (or in the old language *domain* or *partition*) systems. But one never virtualizes a system into four separate domains and ends up with more system processing power and throughput than if you had just purchased four systems equivalent to the size of each domain. Remember that the virtualization software has to use CPU cycles to run and that it's getting those cycles from somewhere. Again, there are many reasons to virtualize, but greater system capacity in a larger domained system as compared to smaller equivalently sized systems is a fallacy and is not one of them.

What are the other reasons we might want to use commodity systems as compared to more costly systems? We are planning to scale aggressively and there are economies to our rate of scaling. We can more easily negotiate for commodity systems. While we might have more of them, it is easier to discard them and work on them at our leisure than the more expensive systems that will demand time. While this may seem counterintuitive, we have been successful in managing more systems with less staff in the commodity (goldfish) world than in the costly system (thoroughbred) world. We pay less for maintenance on these systems, can afford more redundancy, and they fail less often due to fewer parts (CPUs, for example) on a per-unit basis.

And, ultimately, we come to why we call these things "goldfish." At scale, these systems are very inexpensive. If they "die," you are probably incented to simply throw them away rather than investing a lot of time to fix them. "Thoroughbreds" on the other hand represent a fairly large investment that will take time to maintain and fix. Ultimately, we prefer to have many little friends rather than a few big friends.

Rule 12—Scale Out Your Data Centers

Rule 12: What, When, How, and Why

What: Design your systems to have three or more live data centers to reduce overall cost, increase availability, and implement disaster recovery.

When to use: Any rapidly growing business that is considering adding a disaster recovery (cold site) data center.

How to use: Split up your data to spread across data centers and spread transaction load across those data centers in a "multiple live" configuration. Use spare capacity for peak periods of the year.

Why: The cost of data center failure can be disastrous to your business. Design to have three or more as the cost is often less than having two data centers. Make use of idle capacity for peak periods rather than slowing down your transactions.

Key takeaways: When implementing disaster recovery, lower your cost of disaster recovery by designing your systems to leverage three or more live data centers. Use the spare capacity for spiky demand when necessary.

The data center has become one of the biggest pain points in scaling for rapidly growing companies. This is because data centers take a long time to plan and build out and because they are often one of the last things that we think about during periods of rapid growth. And sometimes that "last thing" that we think about is the thing that endangers our company most. This rule is a brief treatment of the "how" and "why" to split up data centers for rapid growth.

First, let's review a few basics. For the purposes of fault isolation (which helps create high availability) and transaction growth, we are going to want to segment our data using both the Y and Z axes of scale presented in Rules 8 and 9, respectively. For the purposes of high availability and transaction growth, we are going to want to replicate (or clone) data and services along the X axis as described in Rule 7. Finally, we are going to assume that you've attempted to apply Rule 40 and that you either have a stateless system or that you can design around your stateful needs to allow for multiple data centers. It is this segmentation, replication, and cloning of data and services as well as *statelessness* that are the building blocks for us to spread our data centers across multiple sites and geographies.

If we have sliced our data properly along the Z axis (see Rule 9), we can now potentially locate data closer to the users requesting that data. If we can slice data while maintaining multitenancy by individual users, we can choose data center locations that are near our end users. If the "atomic" or "granular" element is a company, then we might also locate next to the companies we serve (or at least the largest employee bases of those companies if it is a large company).

Let's start with three data centers. Each data center is the "home" for roughly 33% of our data. We will call these data sets A, B, and C. Each data set in each data center has its data replicated in halves, 50% going to each peer data center. Assuming a Z axis split (see Rule 9) and X axis (see Rule 7) replication of data, 50% of data center A's customers would exist in data center B, and 50% would exist in data center C. In the event of any data center failure, 50% of the data and associated transactions of the data center that failed will move to its peer data centers. If data center A fails, 50% of its data and transactions will go to data center B and 50% to data center C. This approach is depicted in Figure 3.2. The result is that you have 200% of the data necessary to run the site in aggregate, but each site only contains

66% of the necessary data as each site contains the copy for which it is a master (33% of the data necessary to run the site) and 50% of the copies of each of the other sites (16.5% of the data necessary to run the site for a total of an additional 33%).

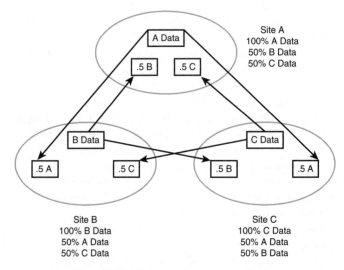

Figure 3.2   Split of data center replication

To see why this configuration is better than the alternative, let's look at some math. Implicit in our assumption is that you agree that you need at least two data centers to stay in business in the event of a geographically isolated disaster. If we have two data centers labeled "A" and "B" you might decide to operate 100% of your traffic out of data center A and leave data center B for a warm standby. In a hot/cold (or active/passive) configuration you would need 100% of your computing and network assets in both data centers to include 100% of your Web and application servers, 100% of your database servers, and 100% of your network equipment. Power needs would be similar and Internet connectivity would be similar. You probably keep slightly more than 100% of the capacity necessary to serve your peak demand in each location to handle surges in demand. So let's say that you keep 110% of your needs in both locations. Anytime you buy additional servers for one place, you have to buy them for the next. You may also decide to connect the data centers with your own dedicated circuits for the purposes of secure replication of data. Running live out of both sites would help you in the event of a major catastrophe as only 50% of your transactions would initially fail until you transfer that traffic to the alternate site, but it won't help you from a budget or financial perspective. A high-level diagram of the data centers may look as depicted in Figure 3.3.

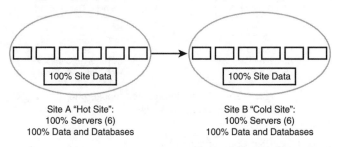

Site A "Hot Site":
100% Servers (6)
100% Data and Databases

Site B "Cold Site":
100% Servers (6)
100% Data and Databases

Figure 3.3   Two data center configuration,
"hot and cold" site

But with three live sites, our costs go down. This is because for all nondatabase systems we only really need 150% of our capacity in each location to run 100% of our traffic in the event of a site failure. For databases, we still need 200% of the storage, but that cost stays with us no matter what approach we use. Power and facilities consumption should also be at roughly 150% of the need for a single site, though obviously we will need slightly more people, and there's probably slightly more overhead than 150% to handle three sites versus one. The only area that increases disproportionately are the network interconnects as we need two additional connections (versus 1) for three sites versus two. Our new data center configuration is shown in Figure 3.4, and the associated comparative operating costs are listed in Table 3.1.

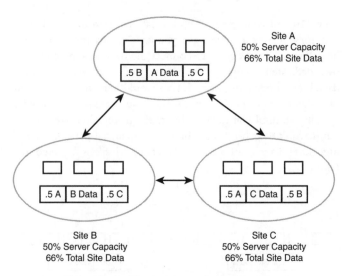

Figure 3.4   Three data center configuration,
three hot sites

Table 3.1   **Cost Comparisons**

Site Configuration	Network	Servers	Data-bases	Storage	Network Site Connections	Total Cost
Single Site	100%	100%	100%	100%	0	100%
2 Site "Hot" and "Cold"	200%	200%	200%	200%	1	200%
2 Site Live/Live	200%	200%	200%	200%	1	200%
3 Site Live/Live/Live	150%	150%	150%	200%	3	~166%

One great benefit out of such a configuration is the ability to leverage our idle capacity for the creation of testing zones (such as load and performance tests) and the ability to leverage these idle assets during spikes in demand. These spikes can come at nearly anytime. Perhaps we get some exceptional and unplanned press, or maybe we just get some incredible viral boost from an exceptionally well-connected individual or company. The capacity we have on hand for a disaster starts getting traffic, and we quickly order additional capacity. Voila!

As we've hinted, running three or more sites comes with certain drawbacks. While the team gains confidence that each site will work as all of them are live, there is some additional operational complexity in running three sites. We believe that, while some additional complexity exists, it is not significantly greater than attempting to run a hot and cold site. Keeping two sites in sync is tough, especially when the team likely doesn't get many opportunities to prove that one of the two sites would actually work if needed. Constantly running three sites is a bit tougher, but not significantly so.

Network transit costs also increase at a fairly rapid pace even as other costs ultimately decline. For a fully connected graph of sites, each new site (N+1) requires N additional connections where N is the previous number of sites. Companies that handle this cost well typically negotiate for volume discounts and play third-party transit providers off of each other for reduced cost.

Finally, we expect to see an increase in employee and employee related costs with a multiple live site model. If our sites are large, we may decide to collocate employees near the sites rather than relying on remote-hands work. Even without employees on site, we will likely need to travel to the sites from time to time to validate setups, work with third-party providers, and so on. The "Multiple Live Site Considerations" sidebar summarizes the benefits, drawbacks, and architectural considerations of a multiple live site implementation.

Multiple Live Site Considerations

Multiple live site benefits include

- Higher availability as compared to a hot and cold site configuration
- Lower costs compared to a hot and cold site configuration
- Faster customer response times if customers are routed to the closest data center for dynamic calls
- Greater flexibility in rolling out products in a SaaS environment
- Greater confidence in operations versus a hot and cold site configuration
- Fast and easy "on-demand" growth for spikes using spare capacity in each data center

Drawbacks or concerns of a multiple live site configuration include

- Greater operational complexity
- Likely a small increase in head count
- Increase in travel and network costs

Architectural considerations in moving to a multiple live site environment include

- Eliminate the need for state and affinity wherever possible
- Route customers to closest data center if possible to reduce dynamic call times
- Investigate replication technologies for databases and state if necessary

Rule 13—Design to Leverage the Cloud

Rule 13: What, When, How, and Why

What: This is the purposeful utilization of cloud technologies to scale on demand.

When to use: When demand is temporary, spiky, and inconsistent and when response time is not a core issue in the product.

How to use:

- Make use of third-party cloud environments for temporary demands, such as large batch jobs or QA environments during testing cycles.
- Design your application to service some requests from a third-party cloud when demand exceeds a certain peak level.

Why: Provisioning of hardware in a cloud environment takes a few minutes as compared to days or weeks for physical servers in your own collocation facility. When utilized temporarily this is also very cost effective.

Key takeaways: Design to leverage virtualization and the cloud to meet unexpected spiky demand.

Cloud computing is part of the infrastructure as a service offering provided by many vendors such as Amazon.com, Inc., Google, Inc., Hewlett-Packard Company, and Microsoft Corporation. Vendor-provided clouds have four primary characteristics: pay by usage, scale on demand, multiple tenants, and virtualization. Third-party clouds are generally comprised of many physical servers that run a hypervisor software allowing them to emulate smaller servers that are called *virtual*. For example, an eight processor machine with 32GB of RAM might be divided into four machines each allowed to utilize two processors and 8GB of RAM.

Customers are allowed to *spin up* or start using one of these virtual servers and are typically charged by how long they use it. Pricing is different for each of the vendors providing these services, but typically the break-even point for utilizing a virtual server versus purchasing a physical server is around 12 months. This means that if you are utilizing the server 24 hours a day for 12 months you will exceed the cost of purchasing the physical server. Where the cost savings arise is that these virtual servers can be started and stopped on demand. Thus, if you only need this server for 6 hours per day for batch processing, your break-even point is extended for upward of 48 months.

While cost is certainly an important factor in your decision to use a cloud, another distinct advantage of the cloud is that provisioning of the hardware typically takes minutes as compared to days or weeks with physical hardware. The approval process required in your company for additional hardware, the steps of ordering, receiving, racking, and loading a server, can easily take weeks. In a cloud environment, additional servers can be brought into service in minutes.

The two ideal ways that we've seen companies make use of third-party cloud environments is when demand is either temporary or inconsistent. Temporary demand can come in the form of nightly batch jobs that need intensive computational resources for a couple of hours or from QA cycles that occur for a couple days each month when testing the next release. Inconsistent demand can come in the form of promotions or seasonality such as "Cyber Monday."

One of our clients makes great use of a third-party cloud environment each night when they process the day's worth of data into their data warehouse. They spin up hundreds of virtual instances, process the data, and then shut them down ensuring they only pay for the amount of computational resources that they need. Another of our clients uses virtual instances for their QA engineers. They build a machine image of the software version to be tested and then as QA engineers need a new environment or refreshed environment, they allocate a new virtual instance. By utilizing virtual instances for their QA environment, the dozens of testing servers don't remain unused the majority of the time. Yet another of our clients utilizes a cloud environment for ad serving when their demand exceeds a certain point. By synchronizing a data store every few minutes, the ads served from the cloud are nearly as up to date as those served from the collocation facility. This particular application can handle a slight delay in the synchronization of data because serving an ad when requested, even if not the absolutely best one, is still much better than not serving the ad because of scaling issues.

Think about your system and what parts are most ideally suited for a cloud environment. Often there are components, such as batch processing, testing environments, or surge capacity, that make sense to put in a cloud. Cloud environments allow for scaling on demand with very short notice.

Summary

While scaling up is an appropriate choice for slow to moderate growth companies, those companies whose growth consistently exceeds Moore's Law will find themselves hitting the computational capacity limits of high-end, very expensive systems with little notice. Nearly all the high-profile services failures about which we've all read have been a result of products simply outgrowing their "britches." We believe it is always wise to plan to scale out early such that when the demand comes, you can easily split up systems. Follow our rules of scaling out both your systems and your data centers, leveraging the cloud for unexpected demand and relying on inexpensive commodity hardware and you will be ready for hyper growth when it comes!

Endnotes

1. Manek Dubash, "Moore's Law is dead, says Gordon Moore,"
    TechWorld, April 13, 2005, www.techworld.com/opsys/news/
    index.cfm?NewsID=3477.

4

Use the Right Tools

You may never have heard of Abraham Maslow, but there is a good chance that you know of his "law of the instrument," otherwise known as Maslow's hammer. Paraphrased, it goes something like "When all you have is a hammer, everything looks like a nail." There are at least two important implications of this "law."

The first is that we all tend to use instruments or tools with which we are familiar in solving the problems before us. If you are a C programmer, you will likely try to solve a problem or implement requirements within C. If you are a DBA, there is a good chance that you'll think in terms of how to use a database to solve a given problem. If your job is to maintain a third-party ecommerce package, you might try to solve nearly any problem using that package rather than simpler solutions that might require a two to three line interpreted shell script.

The second implication of this law really builds on the first. If, within our organizations we consistently bring in people of similar skill sets to solve problems or implement new products, we will very likely get consistent answers built with similar tools and third-party products. The problem with such an approach is that while it has the benefit of predictability and consistency, it may very well drive us to use tools or solutions that are inappropriate or suboptimal for our task. Let's imagine we have a broken sink. Given Maslow's hammer, we would beat on it with our hammer and likely cause further damage. Extending this to our topic of scalability, why would we want to use a database when just writing to a file might be a better solution? Why would we want to implement a firewall if we are only going to block certain ports and we have that ability within our routers? Let's look at a few scalability related "tools rules."

Rule 14—Use Databases Appropriately

Rule 14: What, When, How, and Why

What: Use relational databases when you need ACID properties to maintain relationships between your data. For other data storage needs consider more appropriate tools.

When to use: When you are introducing new data or data structures into the architecture of a system.

How to use: Consider the data volume, amount of storage, response time requirements, relationships, and other factors to choose the most appropriate storage tool.

Why: An RDBMS provides great transactional integrity but is more difficult to scale, costs more, and has lower availability than many other storage options.

Key takeaways: Use the right storage tool for your data. Don't get lured into sticking everything in a relational database just because you are comfortable accessing data in a database.

Relational database management systems (RDBMSs), such as Oracle and MySQL, are based on the relational model introduced by Edgar F. Codd in his 1970 paper "A Relational Model of Data for Large Shared Data Banks." Most RDBMSs provide two huge benefits for storing data. The first is the guarantee of transactional integrity through ACID properties, see Table 2.1 in Chapter 2, "Distribute Your Work," for definitions. The second is the relational structure within and between tables. To minimize data redundancy and improve transaction processing, the tables of most Online Transaction Processing databases (OLTP) are normalized to Third Normal Form, where all records of a table have the same fields, nonkey fields cannot be described by only one of the keys in a composite key, and all nonkey fields must be described by the key. Within the table each piece of data is highly related to other pieces of data. Between tables there are often relationships known as foreign keys. While these are two of the major benefits of using an RDBMS, these are also the reason for their limitations in terms of scalability.

Because of this guarantee of ACID properties, an RDBMS can be more challenging to scale than other data stores. When you guarantee consistency of data and you have multiple nodes in your RDBMS cluster, such as with MySQL NDB, synchronous replication is used to guarantee that data is written to multiple nodes upon committing the data. With Oracle RAC there is a central database, but ownership of areas of the DB are shared among the nodes so write requests have to transfer ownership to that node and reads have to hop from requestor to master to owner and back. Eventually you are limited by the number of nodes that data can be synchronously replicated to or by their physical geographical location.

The relational structure within and between tables in the RDBMS makes it difficult to split the database through such actions as sharding or partitioning. See Chapter 2 for rules related to distributing work across multiple machines. A simple query that joined two tables in a single database must be converted into two separate queries with the joining of the data taking place in the application to split tables into different databases.

The bottom line is that data that requires transactional integrity or relationships with other data are likely ideal for an RDBMS. Data that requires neither relationships with other data nor transactional integrity might be better suited for other storage systems. Let's talk briefly about a few of the alternative storage solutions and how they might be used in place of a database for some purposes to achieve better, more cost-effective, and more scalable results.

One often overlooked storage system is a file system. Perhaps this is thought of as unsophisticated because most of us started programming by accessing data in files rather than databases. Once we graduated to storing and retrieving data from a database we never looked back. File systems have come a long way, and many are specifically designed to handle very large amounts of files and data. Some of these include Google File System (GFS), MogileFS, and Ceph. File systems are great alternatives

when you have a "write once-read many" system. Put another
way, if you don't expect to have conflicting reads and writes over
time on a structure or object and you don't need to maintain a
great deal of relationships, you don't really need the transactional
overhead of a database; file systems are a great choice for this
kind of work.

The next set of alternative storage strategies is termed
NoSQL. Technologies that fall into this category are often
subdivided into key-value stores, extensible record stores, and
document stores. There is no universally agreed classification of
technologies, and many of them could accurately be placed in
multiple categories. We've included some example technologies
in the following descriptions, but this is not to be considered
gospel. Given the speed of development on many of these projects, the classifications are likely to become even more blurred in
the future.

Key-value stores include technologies such as Memcached,
Tokyo Tyrant, and Voldemort. These products have a single key-
value index for data and that is stored in memory. Some have
the capability to write to disk for persistent storage. Some products in this subcategory use synchronous replication across nodes
while others are asynchronous. These offer significant scaling and
performance by utilizing a simplistic data store model, the key-
value pair, but this is also a significant limitation in terms of
what data can be stored. Additionally, the key-value stores that
rely on synchronous replication still face the limitations that
RDBMS clusters do, which are a limit on the number of nodes
and their geographical locations.

Extensible record stores include technologies such as
Google's proprietary BigTable and Facebook's, now open source,
Cassandra. These products use a row and column data model
that can be split across nodes. Rows are split or sharded on
primary keys, and columns are broken into groups and placed on
different nodes. This method of scaling is similar to the X and Y
axes in the AKF Scale Cube, shown in Figure 2.1 in Chapter 2,
where the X axis split is read replicas, and the Y axis is separating
the tables by services supported. In these products row sharding

is done automatically, but column splitting requires user definitions, similar to how it is performed in an RDBMS. These
products utilize an asynchronous replication providing eventual
consistency. This means that eventually, which may take milliseconds or hours, the data will become consistent across all nodes.

Document stores include technologies such as CouchDB,
Amazon's SimpleDB, and Yahoo's PNUTS. The data model used
in this category is called a "document" but is more accurately
described as a multi-indexed object model. The multi-indexed
object (or "document") can be aggregated into collections of
multi-indexed objects (typically called "domains"). These collections or "domains" in turn can be queried on many different
attributes. Document store technologies do not support ACID
properties; instead, they utilize asynchronous replication, providing an eventually consistent model.

NoSQL solutions limit the number of relationships between
objects or entities to a small number. It is this reduction of relationships that allows for the systems to be distributed across
many nodes and achieve greater scalability while maintaining
transactional integrity and read-write conflict resolution.

As is so often the case, and as you've probably determined
reading the preceding text, there is a tradeoff between scalability
and flexibility within these systems. The degree of relationship
between data entities ultimately drives this tradeoff; as relationships increase, flexibility also increases. This flexibility comes at
an increase in cost and a decrease in the ability to easily scale the
system. Figure 4.1 plots RDBMS, NoSQL, and file systems solutions against both the costs (and limits) to scale the system and
the degree to which relationships are used between data entities.
Figure 4.2 plots flexibility against the degree of relationships
allowed within the system. The result is clear: Relationships
engender flexibility but also create limits to our scale. As such,
we do not want to overuse relational databases but rather choose
a tool appropriate to the task at hand to engender greater scalability of our system.

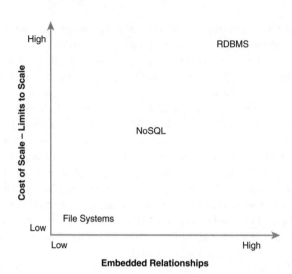

Figure 4.1   Cost and limits to scale versus relationships

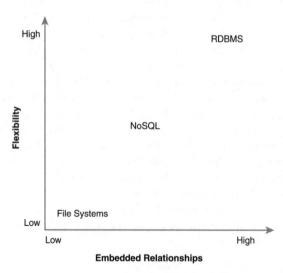

Figure 4.2   Flexibility versus relationships

Another data storage alternative that we are going to cover in this rule is Google's MapReduce.[1] At a high level, MapReduce has both a Map and a Reduce function. The Map function takes a key-value pair as input and produces an intermediate key-value pair. The input key might be the name of a document or pointer to a piece of a document. The value could be content consisting of all the words within the document itself. This output is fed into a reducer function that uses a program that groups the words or parts and appends the values for each into a list. This is a rather trivial program that sorts and groups the functions by key. The huge benefit of this technology is the support of distributed computing of very large data sets across many servers.

An example technology that combines two of our data storage alternatives is Apache's Hadoop. This was inspired by Google's MapReduce and Google File System, both of which are described previously. Hadoop provides benefits of both a highly scalable file system with distributed processing for storage and retrieval of the data.

So now that we've covered a few of the many options that might be preferable to a database when storing data, what data characteristics should you consider when making this decision? As with the myriad of options available for storage, there are numerous characteristics that should be considered. A few of the most important ones are the number of degree of relationships needed between elements, the rate of growth of the solution, and the ratio of reads to writes of the data (and potentially whether data is updated). Finally we are interested in how well the data monetizes (that is, is it profitable?) as we don't want our cost of the system to exceed the value we expect to achieve from it.

The degree of relationships between data is important as it drives flexibility, cost, and time of development of a solution. As an example, imagine the difficulty of storing a transaction involving a user's profile, payment, purchase, and so on, in a key-value store and then retrieving the information piecemeal such as through a report of purchased items. While you can certainly do this with a file system or NoSQL alternative, it may be costly to develop and time consuming in delivering results back to a user.

The expected rate of growth is important for a number of reasons. Ultimately this rate impacts the cost of the system and the response times we would expect for some users. If a high degree of relationships are required between data entities, at some point we will run out of hardware and processing capacity to support a single integrated database, driving us to split the databases into multiple instances.

Read and write ratios are important as they help drive an understanding of what kind of system we need. Data that is written once and read many times can easily be put on a file system coupled with some sort of application, file, or object cache. Images are great examples of systems that typically can be put on file systems. Data that is written and then updated, or with high write to read ratios, are better off within NoSQL or RDBMS solutions.

These considerations bring us to another cube, Figure 4.3, where we've plotted the three considerations against each other. Note that as the X, Y, and Z axes increase in value, so does the cost of the ultimate solution increase. Where we require a high degree of relationships between systems (upper right and back portion of Figure 4.3), rapid growth, and resolution of read and write conflicts we are likely tied to several smaller RDBMS systems at relatively high cost in both our development and the systems, maintenance, and possibly licenses for the databases. If growth and size are small but relationships remain high and we need to resolve read and write conflict, we can use a single monolithic database (with high availability clustering).

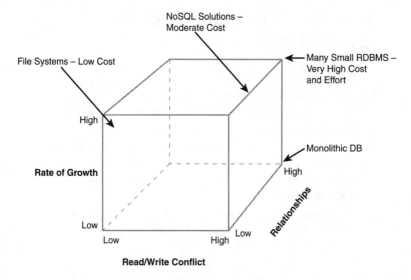

Figure 4.3   Solution decision cube

Relaxing relationships slightly allows us to use NoSQL alternatives at any level of reads and writes and with nearly any level of growth. Here again we see the degree to which relationships drive our cost and complexity, a topic we explore later in Chapter 8, "Database Rules." Cost is lower for these NoSQL alternatives. Finally, where relationship needs are low and read-write conflict is not a concern we can get into low-cost file systems to provide our solutions.

Monetization value of the data is critical to understand because as many struggling startups have experienced, storing terabytes of user data for free on class A storage is a quick way to run out of capital. A much better approach might be using tiers of data storage; as the data ages in terms of access date, continue to push it off to cheaper and slower access storage media. We call this the *Cost-Value Data Dilemma*, which is where the value of data decreases over time and the cost of keeping it increases over time. We discuss this dilemma more in Rule 47 and describe how to solve the dilemma cost effectively.

Rule 15—Firewalls, Firewalls Everywhere!

Rule 15: What, When, How, and Why

What: Use firewalls only when they significantly reduce risk and recognize that they cause issues with scalability and availability.

When to use: Always.

How to use: Employ firewalls for critical PII, PCI compliance, and so on. Don't use them for low-value static content.

Why: Firewalls can lower availability and cause unnecessary scalability chokepoints.

Key takeaways: While firewalls are useful, they are often overused and represent both an availability and scalability concern if not designed and implemented properly.

The decision to employ security measures should ultimately be viewed from the lens of profit maximization. Security in general is an approach to reduce risk. Risk in turn is a function of both the probability that an action will happen and the impact or damage the action causes should it happen. Firewalls help to manage risk in some cases by reducing the probability that an event happens. They do so at some additional capital expense, some impact to availability (and hence either transaction revenue or customer satisfaction), and often an additional area of concern for scalability: the creation of a difficult to scale chokepoint in either network traffic or transaction volume. Unfortunately, far too many companies view firewalls as an all or nothing approach to security. They overuse firewalls and underuse other security approaches that would otherwise make them even more secure. We can't understate the impact of firewalls to availability. In our experience, failed firewalls are the number two driver of site downtime next to failed databases. As such, this rule is about reducing them in number. Remember, however, that there are many other things that you should be doing for security while you look to eliminate any firewalls that are unnecessary or simply burdensome.

In our practice, we view firewalls as perimeter security devices meant to increase both the perceived and actual cost of gaining entry to a product. In this regard, they serve a similar purpose as the locks you have on the doors to your house. In fact, we believe that the house analogy is appropriate to how one should view firewalls, so we'll build on that analogy here.

There are several areas of your house that you don't likely lock up—for example, you probably don't lock up your front yard. You probably also leave certain items of relatively low value in front of your house, such as hoses and gardening implements. You may also leave your vehicle outside even though you know it is more secure in your garage given how quickly most thieves can bypass vehicle security systems. More than likely you have locks and maybe deadbolts on your exterior doors and potentially smaller privacy locks on your bathrooms and bedrooms. Other rooms of your house, including your closets, probably don't have locks on them. Why the differences in our approaches?

Certain areas outside your house, while valuable to you, simply aren't of significant value for someone else to steal them. You really value your front yard but probably don't think someone's going to come with a shovel and dig it up to replant elsewhere. You might be concerned with someone riding a bicycle across it and destroying the grass or the sprinkler head, but that concern probably doesn't drive you to incur the additional cost of fencing it (other than a decorative picket fence) and destroying the view for both you and others within the neighborhood.

Your interior doors really only have locks for the purpose of privacy. Most of the interior doors don't have locks meant to keep out an interested and motivated intruder. We don't lock and deadbolt most of our interior doors because these locks present more of a hassle to us as occupants of the house, and the additional hassle really isn't worth the additional security provided by such locks.

Now consider your product. Several aspects, such as static images, .css files, JavaScript, and so on, are important to you but don't really need high-end security. In many cases, you likely look to deliver these attributes via an edge-cache (or content delivery network) outside your network anyway (see Chapter 6,

"Use Caching Aggressively"). As such, we shouldn't subject these objects to an additional network hop (the firewall), the associated lower overall availability, and its scale limiting attributes of an additional network chokepoint. We can save some money and reduce the load on our firewalls simply by ensuring that these objects are delivered from private IP addresses and only have access via port 80 and 443.

Returning to the value and costs of firewalls, let's explore a framework by which we might decide when and where to implement firewalls. We've indicated that firewalls cost us in the following ways: There is a capital cost to purchase the firewall, they create an additional item that needs to be scaled, and they represent an impact to our availability as it is one more device on the critical route of any transaction that can fail and cause problems. We've also indicated that they add value when they are used to deter or hinder the efforts of those who would want to steal from us or harm our product. Table 4.1 shows a matrix indicating some of the key decision criteria for us in implementing firewalls.

Table 4.1   **Firewall Implementation Matrix**

Value to "Bad Guy"	Cost to Firewall	Examples	Firewall Decision
Low	High	css, static images, JavaScript	No
Low	Medium	product catalogs, search services	No
Medium	Medium	critical business functions	Maybe
High	Low	Personally identifiable information (e.g., social security numbers, credit cards), password reset information	Yes

The first thing that you might notice is that we've represented value to the bad guy and cost to firewall as having a near inverse relationship. While this relationship won't always be true, in many of our clients' products it is the case. Static object references tend to represent a majority of object requests on a page and often are the heaviest elements of the pages. As such they tend to be costly to firewall given the transaction rate and throughput requirements. They are even more costly when you consider that they hold very little value to a potential bad guy. Given the high cost in terms of potential availability impact and capital relative to the likelihood that they are the focus of a bad guy's intentions, it makes little sense for us to invest in their protection. We'll just ensure that they are on private IP space (for example, 10.X.Y.Z addresses or the like) and that the only traffic that gets to them are requests for ports 80 and 443.

On the flip side we have items like credit cards, bank account information, and social security numbers. These items have a high perceived value to our bad guy. They are also less costly to protect relative to other objects as they tend to be requested less frequently than many of our objects. We absolutely should lock these things away!

In the middle are all the other requests that we service within our platform. It probably doesn't make a lot of sense to ensure that every search a user performs goes through a firewall. What are we protecting? The actual servers themselves? We can protect our assets well against attacks such as distributed denial of service attacks with packet filters, routers, and carrier relationships. Other compromises can be thwarted by limiting the ports that access these systems. If there isn't a huge motivation for a bad guy to go after the services, let's not spend a lot of money and decrease our availability by pretending that they are the crown jewels.

In summation, don't assume that everything deserves the same level of protection. The decision to employ firewalls is a business decision focused on decreasing risk at the cost of decreasing availability and increasing capital costs. Too many companies view firewalls as a unary decision—if it exists within our site it must be firewalled when in fact firewalls are just one of many tools you might employ to help decrease your risk. Not everything in your product is likely deserving of the cost and impact to availability that a firewall represents. As with any other business decision, this one should be considered in the light of these tradeoffs, rather than just assuming a cookie-cutter approach to your implementation. Given the nature of firewalls, they can easily become the biggest bottleneck from a scale perspective for your product.

Rule 16—Actively Use Log Files

> ### Rule 16: What, When, How, and Why
>
> **What:** Use your application's log files to diagnose and prevent problems.
>
> **When to use:** Put a process in place that monitors log files and forces people to take action on issues identified.
>
> **How to use:** Use any number of monitoring tools from custom scripts to Splunk to watch your application logs for errors. Export these and assign resources for identifying and solving the issue.
>
> **Why:** The log files are excellent sources of information about how your application is performing for your users; don't throw this resource away without using it.
>
> **Key takeaways:** Make good use of your log files, and you will have fewer production issues with your system.

In the spirit of using the right tools for the job, one of the tools that is likely in all our toolboxes but often gets overlooked are log files. Unless you've purposely turned off logging on your Web or application servers almost all varieties come with error and access logs. Apache has error and access logs, Tomcat has java.util.logging or Log4j logs, and Websphere has SystemErr and SystemOut logs. These logs can be incredibly valuable tools for providing insights into the performance and problems occurring within your application that might prevent it from scaling. To best use this tool there are a few simple but important steps to follow.

The first step in using log files is to aggregate them. As you probably have dozens or perhaps even hundreds of servers, you need to pull this data together to use it. If the amount of data is too large to pull together there are strategies such as sampling, pulling data from every n^{th} server, which can be implemented. Another strategy is to aggregate the logs from a few servers onto a log server that can then transmit the semi-aggregated logs into the final aggregation location. As shown in Figure 4.4, dedicated log servers can aggregate the log data to then be sent to a data store. This aggregation is generally done through an out-of-band network that is not the same network used for production traffic. What we want to avoid is impacting production traffic from logging, monitoring, or aggregating data.

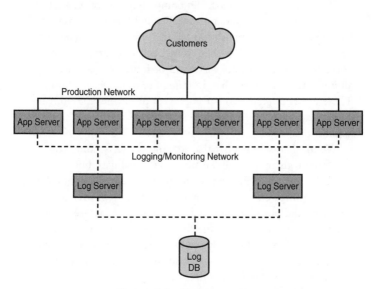

Figure 4.4   Log aggregation

The next step is to monitor these logs. Surprisingly many companies spend the time and computational resources to log and aggregate but then ignore the data. While you can just use log files during incidents to help restore service, this isn't optimal. A preferred use is to monitor these files with automated tools. This monitoring can be done through custom scripts such as a simple shell script that greps the files, counting errors and alerting when a threshold is exceeded. More sophisticated tools such as Cricket or Cacti include graphing capabilities. A tool that combines the aggregation and monitoring of log files is Splunk.

Once you've aggregated the logs and monitored them for errors, the last step is to take action to fix the problems. This requires assigning engineering and QA resources to identify common errors as being related to individual problems. It is often the case that one bug in an application flow can result in many different error manifestations. The same engineers who identified the bug might also get assigned to fix it, or other engineers might get assigned the task.

We'd like to have the log files completely free of errors, but we know that's not always possible. While it's not uncommon to have some errors in application log files you should establish a process that doesn't allow them to get out of control or ignored. Some teams periodically, every third or fourth release, clean up all miscellaneous errors that don't require immediate actions. These errors might be something as simple as missing redirect configurations or not handling known error conditions in the application.

We must also remember that logging comes at some cost. Not only is there a cost in keeping additional data, but very often there is a cost in terms of transaction response times. We can help mitigate the former by summarizing logs over time and archiving and purging them as their value decreases (see Rule 47). We can help minimize the former by logging in an asynchronous fashion. Ultimately we must pay attention to our costs for logging and make a cost-effective decision of both how much to log and how much data to keep.

Hopefully we've convinced you that log files are an important tool in your arsenal of debugging and monitoring your application. By simply using a tool that you likely already have, you can greatly improve your customer experience and scalability of your application.

Summary

Using the right tool for the job is important in any discipline. Just as you wouldn't want your plumber to bring only a hammer into your house to fix your pipes, your customers and investors don't want you to bring a single tool to solve problems with diverse characteristics and requirements. Avoid falling prey to Maslow's hammer and bring together diverse teams capable of thinking of different solutions to problems. A final word of caution on this topic is that each new technology introduced requires another skill set to support. While the right tool for the job is important, don't overspecialize to the point that you have no depth of skills to support your systems.

Endnotes

1. Jeffrey Dean and Sanjay Ghernawat, "Map Reduce: Simplified Data
    Processing on Large Clusters," Google Research Publications,
    http://labs.google.com/papers/mapreduce.html.

5

Don't Duplicate Your Work

No one wants to do the same thing over and over again, unless perhaps you are a professional musician or athlete. For most of us, repetitious work is mind numbing, boring, and tedious. The people who read this book are probably not folks who find personal fulfillment using a torque wrench to drive in the same five screws over and over again every day. Yet, surprisingly, many of us do some seemingly small tasks over and over again to the detriment of the scalability of our platform. The three rules we discuss in this chapter are the three most common drivers of duplicated work and value defeating requirements that we see in our consulting practice day in and day out. Some of them might strike you as obvious or even odd. We entreat you to dig within your organizations and engineering efforts as we suspect that you might find some of these value killers lurking about in the shadows.

Rule 17—Don't Check Your Work

Rule 17: What, When, How, and Why

What: Avoid checking things you just did or reading things you just wrote within your products.

When to use: Always (see rule conflict in the following explanation).

How to use: Never read what you just wrote for the purpose of validation. Store data in a local or distributed cache if it is required for operations in the near future.

Why: The cost of validating your work is high relative to the unlikely cost of failure. Such activities run counter to cost-effective scaling.

Key takeaways: Never justify reading something you just wrote for the purposes of validating the data. Read and act upon errors associated with the write activity instead. Avoid other types of reads of recently written data by storing that data locally.

Carpenters and woodworkers have an expression: "Measure twice and cut once." You might have learned such a phrase from a high school wood shop teacher—one who might have been missing a finger. Missing digits aside, the logic behind such a statement is sound and based on experience through practice. It's much better to validate a measurement before making a cut, as a failed measurement will potentially increase production waste by creating a useless board of the wrong size. We won't argue with such a plan. Instead, we aim to eliminate waste of a different kind: the writing and subsequent immediate validation of the just-written data.

We've been surprised over the last several years at how often we find ourselves asking our clients "What do you mean you are reading and validating something that you just wrote?" Sometimes clients have a well thought out reason for their actions, though we have yet to see one with which we agree. More often than not, the client cops a look that reminds us of a child who just got caught doing something he or she knew should not be done. The claims of those with well thought out (albeit in our opinion value destroying) answers are that their

application requires an absolute guarantee that the data not only
be written but also be written correctly. Keep in mind that most
of our clients have SaaS or commerce platforms—they aren't
running nuclear power facilities, sending people into space,
controlling thousands of passenger-laden planes in flight, or
curing cancer. Fear of failed writes and calculations has long
driven extra effort on the part of many a developer. This fear,
perhaps justified in the dark ages of computing, was at least
partially responsible for the fault-tolerant computer designs
developed by both Tandem and Stratus in the late 1970s and
early 1980s, respectively. The primary driver of these systems was
to reduce mean time to failure (MTTF) within systems through
"redundant everything" including CPUs, storage, memory,
memory paths, storage paths, and so on. Some models of these
computers necessarily compared results of computations and
storage operations along parallel paths to validate that the systems were working properly. One of the authors of this book
developed applications for an aging Stratus minicomputer, and in
the two years he worked with it, the system never identified a
failure in computation between the two processors, or failure
writes to memory or disk.

Today those fears are much less founded than they were in the
late 1970s through the late 1980s. In fact, when we ask our clients
who first write something and then attempt to immediately read
it how often they find failures, the answer is fairly consistent:
"Never." And the chances are that unless they fail to act upon an
error returned from a write operation, they will never experience
such an event. Sure, corruption happens from time to time, but in
most cases that corruption is identified during the actual write
operation. Rather than doubling your activities, thereby halving
the number of transactions you can perform on your storage,
databases, and systems, simply look at the error codes returned
from your operations and react accordingly. As a side note here,
the most appropriate protection against corruption is to properly
implement high availability and have multiple copies of data
around such as a standby database or replicated storage (see
Chapter 9, "Design for Fault Tolerance and Graceful Failure").
Ideally you will ultimately implement multiple live sites (see
Chapter 3, "Design to Scale Out Horizontally," Rule 12).

Of course not every "write then immediately read" activity is a result of an overzealous engineer attempting to validate what he or she has just written. Sometimes it's the result of an end user immediately requesting the thing they just wrote. The question we ask here is why these clients don't store frequently used (including written) data locally? If you just wrote something and you know you are likely to need it again, just keep it around locally. One common example of such a need is during a registration flow for most products. Typically there is a stage at which one wants to present to the user the data you are about to commit to the permanent registration "record." Another one might be the purchase flow embedded within most shopping cart systems on commerce sites. Regardless of the case, it makes sense to keep around the information you are writing if it is going to be needed in the future. Storing and then immediately fetching is just a wasteful use of system resources. See Chapter 6, "Use Caching Aggressively," for more information on how and what to cache.

The point to which all the preceding paragraphs are leading up to is that doubling your activity reduces your ability to scale cost effectively. In fact, it doubles your cost for those transactions. So while you may be engineering a solution to avoid a couple of million in risk associated with failed writes, you may be incurring tens of millions of dollars in extra infrastructure to accomplish it. Rarely, and in our experience never, does this investment in engineering time and infrastructure overcome the risk it mitigates. Reading after writing is bad in most cases because it not only doubles your cost and limits your scalability, it rarely returns value in risk mitigation commensurate with the costs. There are no doubt cases where it is warranted, though those are far fewer in number than justified by many technology teams and businesses.

The observant reader may have identified a conflict in our rules. Storing information locally on a system might be indicative of state and certainly requires affinity to the server to be effective. As such, we've violated Rule 40. At a high level, we agree, and if forced to make a choice we would always develop a stateless application over ensuring that we don't have to read

what we just wrote. That said, our rules are meant to be nomo-
thetic or "generally true" rather than idiographic or "specifically
true." You should absolutely try not to duplicate your work and
absolutely try to maintain a largely stateless application. Are these
two statements sometimes in conflict? Yes. Is that conflict resolv-
able? Absolutely!

The way we resolve such a conflict in rules is to take the
30,000 foot approach. We want a system that does not waste
resources (like reading what we just wrote) while we attempt to
be largely stateless for reasons we discuss in Chapter 10, "Avoid
or Distribute State." To do this, we decide to never read for the
sake of validation. We also agree that there are times when we
might desire affinity for speed and scale versus reading what we
just wrote. This means maintaining some notion of state, but we
limit these to transactions where it is necessary for us to read
something that we just wrote. While this approach causes a vio-
lation of our state rules, it makes complete sense as we are
attempting to introduce state in a limited set of operations
where it actually decreases cost and increases scalability as
opposed to how it often does just the opposite.

As with any rule, there are likely exceptions. What if you exist
in a regulatory environment that requires absolutely 100% of all
writes of a particular piece of data be verified to exist, encrypt-
ed, and backed up? We're not certain such an environment exists,
but if it did there are almost always ways to meet requirements
such as these without blocking for an immediate read of data
that was just written. Here is a bulleted checklist of questions
you can answer and steps you can take to eliminate reading what
you just wrote and blocking the user transaction to do so:

- **Regulatory/legal requirement**—Is this activity a regulatory or legal requirement? If it is, are you certain that
  you have read it properly? Rarely does a requirement spell
  out that you need to do something "in line" with a user
  transaction. And even if it does, the requirement rarely
  (probably never) applies to absolutely everything that
  you do.

- **Competitive differentiation**—Does this activity provide
  competitive differentiation? Careful—"Yes" is an all-too-
  common and often incorrect answer to this question.

Given the small rate of failures you would expect, it is hard to believe that you will win by correctly handling the .001% of failures that your competitors will have by not checking twice.

- **Asynchronous completion**—If you have to read after writing for the purposes of validation due to either a regulatory requirement (doubtful but possible) or competitive differentiation (beyond doubtful—see above), then consider doing it asynchronously. Write locally and do not block the transaction. Handle any failures to process by re-creating the data from logs, reapplying it from a processing queue or worst case asking the user for it again in the very small percentage of cases where you lose it. If the failure is in copying the data to a remote backup for high availability, simply reapply that record or transaction. Never block the user under any scenario pending a synchronous write to two data sources.

Rule 18—Stop Redirecting Traffic

Rule 18: What, When, How, and Why

What: Avoid redirects when possible; use the right method when they are necessary.

When to use: Use redirects as little as possible.

How to use: If you must have them, consider server configurations instead of HTML or other code-based solutions.

Why: Redirects in general delay the user, consume computation resources, and are prone to errors.

Key takeaways: Use redirects correctly and only when necessary.

There are many reasons that you might want to redirect traffic. A few of these include tracking clicks on content or an advertisement, misspelled domains (for example, a*fk*partners.com instead of a*kf*partners.com), aliasing or shortening URLs (for example, akfpartners.com/news instead of akfpartners.com/news/index.php), or changing domains (for example, moving the site from akf-consulting.com to akfpartners.com). There is even a design pattern called Post/Redirect/Get (PRG) that is used to avoid some duplicated form submissions. Essentially this pattern calls for the post operation on a form submission to redirect the browser, preferably with an HTTP 303 response. All these and more are valid reasons for redirecting users from one place to another. However, like any good tool it can be used improperly, like trying to use a screwdriver for a hammer, or too frequently, such as splitting a cord of wood without sharpening your axe. Either problem ends up with less than desirable results. Let's first talk a little more about redirection according to the HTTP standard.

According to RFC2616, Hypertext Transfer Protocol,[1] there are several redirect codes, including the more familiar 301 moved permanently and the 302 found for temporary redirection. These codes fall under the Redirection 3xx heading and refer to a class of status code that requires further action to be taken by the user agent to fulfill the request. The complete list of 3xx codes is provided in the following sidebar.

HTTP 3xx Status Codes

- **300 Multiple Choices**—The requested resource corresponds to any one of many representations and is being provided so that the user can select a preferred representation.

- **301 Moved Permanently**—The requested resource has been assigned a new permanent URI, and any future references to this resource *should* use the URI returned.

- **302 Found**—The requested resource resides temporarily under a different URI, but the client *should* continue to use the Request-URI for future requests.

- **303 See Other**—The response to the request can be found under a different URI and *should* be retrieved using a GET method. This method exists primarily for the PRG design pattern to allow the output of a POST to redirect the user agent.

- **304 Not Modified**—If the client has performed a conditional GET request and access is allowed, but the document has not been modified, the server *should* respond with this status code.

- **305 Use Proxy**—The requested resource *must* be accessed through the proxy given by the Location field.

- **306 (Unused)**—This status code is no longer used in the specification.

- **307 Temporary Redirect**—The requested resource resides temporarily under a different URI.

So, we've agreed that there are many valid reasons for using redirects and the HTTP standard even has multiple status codes that allow for various types of redirects. What then is the problem with redirects? The problem is that they can be performed in numerous ways, some better than others in terms of resource utilization and performance, and they can easily get out of hand. Let's examine a few of the most popular methods of redirecting users from one URI to another and discuss the pros and cons of each.

The simplest way to redirect a user from one page or domain to another is to construct an HTML page that requests they click on a link to proceed to the real resources they are attempting to retrieve. The page might look something like this:

```
<html><head></head><body>
 <p>Please click <a href="http://www.akfpartners.com/
techblog">here for your requested page</a></p>
</body></html>
```

The biggest problem with this method is that it requires the user to click again to retrieve the real page he was after. A slightly better way to redirect with HTML is to use the meta tag "refresh" and automatically send the user's browser to the new page. The HTML code for that would look like this:

```
<html><head>
 <meta http-equiv="Refresh" content="0;
url=http://www.akfpartners.com/techblog" />
</head><body>
 <p>In case your page doesn't automatically refresh, click
<a href="http://www.akfpartners.com/techblog">here for your
requested page</a></p>
</body></html>
```

With this we solved the user interaction problem, but we're still wasting resources by requiring our Web server to receive a request and respond with a page back to the browser that must parse the HTML code before the redirection. Another more sophisticated method of handling redirects is through code. Almost all languages allow for redirects; in PHP the code might look like this.

```
<?
Header( "HTTP/1.1 301 Moved Permanently" );
Header( "Location: http://www.akfpartners.com/techblog" );
?>
```

This code has the benefit of not requiring the browser to parse HTML but rather redirect through an HTTP status code in a header field. In HTTP, header fields contain the operating parameters of a request or response by defining various characteristics of the data transfer. The PHP preceding code results in the following response:

```
HTTP/1.1 301 Moved Permanently
Date: Mon, 11 Oct 2010 19:39:39 GMT
Server: Apache/2.2.9 (Fedora)
X-Powered-By: PHP/5.2.6
Location: http://www.akfpartners.com/techblog
Cache-Control: max-age=3600
Expires: Mon, 11 Oct 2010 20:39:39 GMT
Vary: Accept-Encoding,User-Agent
Content-Type: text/html; charset=UTF-8
```

We've now improved our redirection by using HTTP status codes in the header fields, but we're still requiring our server to interpret the PHP script. Instead of redirecting in code, which requires either interpretation or execution, we can request the server to redirect for us with its own embedded module. In the Apache Web server two primary modules are used for redirecting, `mod_alias` or `mod_rewrite`. The `mod_alias` is the easiest to understand and implement but is not terribly sophisticated in what it can accomplish. This module can implement `alias`, `aliasmatch`, `redirect`, or `redirectmatch` commands. Following is an example of a `mod_alias` entry:

```
Alias /image /www/html/image
Redirect /service http://foo2.akfpartners.com/service
```

The `mod_rewrite` module compared to the `mod_alias` module is sophisticated. According to Apache's own documentation this module is a "killer one"[2] because it provides a powerful way to manipulate URLs, but the price you pay is increased complexity. An example rewrite entry for redirecting all requests for *artofscale.com* or *www.artofscale.com* URLs to *theartofscalability.com* permanently (301 status code) follows:

```
RewriteEngine on
RewriteCond %{HTTP_HOST} ^artofscale.com$ [OR]
RewriteCond %{HTTP_HOST} ^www.artofscale.com$
RewriteRule ^/?(.*)$
"http\:\/\/theartofscalability\.com\/$1" [R=301,L]
```

To add to the complexity, Apache allows the scripts for these modules to be placed in either the .htaccess files or the httpd.conf main configuration file. However, using the .htaccess files should be avoided in favor of the main configuration files primarily because of performance.[3] When configured to allow the use of .htaccess files, Apache looks in every directory for .htaccess files, thus causing a performance hit, whether you use them or not! Also, the .htaccess file is loaded every time a document is requested instead of once at startup like the httpd.conf main configuration file.

We've now seen some pros and cons of redirecting through different methods, which hopefully will guide us in how to use redirection as a tool. The last topic to cover is making sure you're using the right tool in the first place. Ideally we want to avoid redirection completely. A few of the reasons to avoid redirection when possible is that it always delays the user from getting the resource she wants, it takes up computational resources, and there are many ways to mess up redirection hurting user browsing or search engine rankings.

A few examples of ways that redirects can be wrong come directly from Google's page on why URLs are not followed by its search engine bots.[4] These include redirect errors, redirect loops, too long URLs, and empty redirects. You might think that creating a redirect loop would be difficult, but it is much easier than you think, and while most browsers and bots stop when they detect the loop, it takes up a ton of resources trying to service those requests.

As we mentioned in the beginning of this rule there are certainly times when redirection is necessary, but with a little thought there are ways around many of these. Take click tracking for example. There are certainly all types of business needs to keep track of clicks, but there might be a better way than sending the user to a server to record the click in an access log or application log and then sending the user to the desired site. One alternative is in the browser to use the onClick event handler to call a JavaScript function. This function can request a 1x1 pixel through a PHP or other script that records the click. The beauty of this solution is that it doesn't require the user's browser to request a page, receive back a page or even a header, before it can start loading the desired page.

When it comes to redirects, make sure you first think through ways that you can avoid them. Using the right tool for the job as discussed in Chapter 4, "Use the Right Tools," is important, and redirects are specialized tools. Once those options fail, consider how best to use the redirect tool. We covered several methods and discussed their pros and cons. The specifics of your application will dictate the best alternative.

Rule 19—Relax Temporal Constraints

Rule 19: What, When, How, and Why

What: Alleviate temporal constraints in your system whenever possible.

When to use: Any time you are considering adding a constraint that an item or object maintains a certain state between a user's actions.

How to use: Relax constraints in the business rules.

Why: The difficulty in scaling systems with temporal constraints is significant because of the ACID properties of most RDBMSs.

Key takeaways: Carefully consider the need for constraints such as items being available from the time a user views them until the user purchases them. Some possible edge cases where users are disappointed are much easier to compensate for than not being able to scale.

In the domains of mathematics and machine learning (artificial intelligence) there is a set of Constraint Satisfaction Problems (CSP) where the state of a set of objects must satisfy certain constraints. CSPs are often highly complex, requiring a combination of heuristics and combinatorial search methods to be solved.[5] Two classic puzzles that can be modeled as CSPs are Sudoku and the map coloring problem. The goal of Sudoku is to fill each nine-square row, each nine-square column, and each nine-square box with the numbers 1 through 9, with each number used once and only once in each section. The goal of a map coloring problem is to color a map so that regions sharing a common border have different colors. Solving this involves representing the map as a graph where each region is a vertex and an edge connects two vertices if the corresponding regions share a border.

A more specific variety of the CSP is a Temporal Constraint Satisfaction Problem (TCSP), which is a representation where variables denote events, and constraints represent the possible temporal relations between them. The goals are ensuring consistency among the variables and determining scenarios that satisfy all constraints. Enforcing what is known as local consistency on the variables ensures that the constraints are satisfied for all nodes, arcs, and paths within the problem. While many problems within machine learning and computer science can be modeled as TCSPs, including machine vision, scheduling, and floor plan design, use cases within SaaS systems can also be thought of as TCSPs.

An example of a temporal constraint within a typical SaaS application would be purchasing an item in stock. There are time lapses between a user viewing an item, putting it in his shopping cart, and purchasing it. One could argue that for the absolute best user experience, the state of the object, whether or not it is available, would ideally remain consistent throughout this process. To do so would require that the application mark the item as "taken" in the database until the user browses off the page, abandons the cart, or makes the purchase.

This is pretty straightforward until we get a lot of users on our site. It's not uncommon for users to view 100 or more items before they add anything to their cart. One of our clients claims that users look at more than 500 search results before adding a single item to their cart. In this case our application probably needs several read replicas of the database to allow many more people to search and view items than to purchase them. Herein lies the problem; most RDBMSs aren't good at keeping all the data completely consistent between nodes. Even though read replicas or slave databases can be kept within seconds of each other in terms of consistent data, certainly there will be edge cases when two users want to view the last available inventory of a particular item. We'll come back and solve this problem, but first let's talk about why databases make this difficult.

In Chapter 2, "Distribute Your Work," and Chapter 4, "Use the Right Tools," we spoke about ACID properties of RDBMSs (refer to Table 2.1). The one property that makes scaling an RDBMS in a distributed manner difficult is consistency. The CAP Theorem, also known as the Brewer Theorem so named after computer scientist Eric Brewer, states that three core requirements exist when designing applications in a distributed environment, but it is impossible to simultaneously satisfy all three requirements. These requirements are expressed in the acronym CAP:

- Consistency—The client perceives that a set of operations has occurred all at once.

- Availability—Every operation must terminate in an intended response.

- Partition tolerance—Operations will complete, even if individual components are unavailable.

What has been derived as a solution to this problem is called BASE, an acronym for architectures that solve CAP and stands for Basically Available, Soft State, and Eventually Consistent. By relaxing the ACID properties of consistency we have greater flexibility in how we scale. A BASE architecture allows for the databases to become consistent, eventually. This might be minutes or even just seconds, but as we saw in the previous example, even milliseconds of inconsistency can cause problems if our application expects to be able to "lock" the data.

The way we would redesign our system to accommodate this eventual consistency would be to relax the temporal constraint. The user just viewing an item would not guarantee that it was available. The application would "lock" the data when it was placed into a shopping cart, and this would be done on the primary write copy or master database. Because we have ACID properties we can guarantee that if our transaction completes and we mark the record of the item as "locked," then that user can continue through the purchase confident that the item is reserved for them. Other users viewing the item may or may not have it available for them to purchase.

Another area in which temporal constraints are commonly found in applications is the transfer of items (money) or communications between users. Guaranteeing that user A gets the money, message, or item in her account as soon as user B sends it is easy on a single database. Spreading out the data among several copies of the data makes this consistency much more difficult. The way to solve this is to not expect or require the temporal constraint of instant transfer. More than likely it is totally acceptable that user A wait a few seconds before she sees the money that user B sent. The reason is simply that most dyads don't synchronously transfer items in a system. Obviously synchronous communication such as chat is different.

It is easy to place temporal constraints on your system because at first glance it appears that it would be the best customer experience to do so. However, before doing so consider the long-term ramifications of how difficult that system will be to scale because of the constraint.

Summary

We offered three rules in this chapter that deal with not duplicating your work. Start by not double checking yourself. You employ expensive databases and hardware to ensure your systems properly record transactions and events. Don't expect them *not* to work. We all have the need for redirection at times, but excessive use of this tool causes all types of problems from user experience to search engine indexing. Finally, consider the business requirements that you place on your system. Temporal constraints of items and objects make it difficult and expensive to scale. Carefully consider the real costs and benefits of these decisions.

Endnotes

1. R. Fielding et al., Networking Working Group Request for Comments 2616, "Hypertext Transfer Protocol—HTTP/1.1," June 1999, http://www.w3.org/Protocols/rfc2616/rfc2616.html.
2. Ralf S. Engelschall, "URL Rewriting Guide," Apache HTTP Server Version 2.2, December 1997, http://httpd.apache.org/docs/current/misc/rewriteguide.html.
3. Apache HTTP Server Version 1.3, ".htaccess Files," http://httpd.apache.org/docs/1.3/howto/htaccess.html.
4. Google Webmaster Central, Webmaster Tools Help, "URLs Not Followed Errors," http://www.google.com/support/webmasters/bin/answer.py?answer=35156.
5. Wikipedia, "Constraint satisfaction problem," http://en.wikipedia.org/wiki/Constraint_satisfaction_problem.

6

Use Caching
Aggressively

It is often said in the world of business that "Cash is King." In
the technology world, a close parallel to this saying is the homo-
phone "cache," as in "Cache is King." While we typically tell our
clients that there is a difference between tuning and scaling, and
while we often indicate that caching is more of a tuning activity
than a scaling activity, there is no doubt that the application of
caches "in depth" throughout one's platform architecture has significant impact to the scalability of one's site. By caching at
every level from the browser through the cloud, your network,
application servers, and even databases, one can significantly
increase one's ability to scale. Similar to the theme of Chapter 5,
"Don't Duplicate Your Work," caching is also about how to minimize the amount of work your system does. Caching allows you
to not look up, create, or serve the same data over and over
again. This chapter covers seven rules that will help guide you
on the appropriate type and amount of caching for your
application.

A word of caution is warranted here before we get into these
rules. As with any system implementation or major modification,
the addition of caching, while often warranted, will create complexity within your system. Multiple levels of caching can make
it more difficult to troubleshoot problems in your product. As
such, you should design the caching to be monitored as we
discuss in Rule 49. While caching is a mechanism that often

engenders greater scalability, it also needs to be engineered to
scale well. Developing a caching solution that doesn't scale well
will create a scalability chokepoint within your system and lead
to lower availability down the road. The failure of caches can
have catastrophic impact to the availability of your site as services soon get overloaded. As such, you should ensure that you've
designed the caches to be highly available and easily maintained.
Finally, caching is a bit of an art that is performed best with
deep experience. Look to hire engineers with past experience to
help you with your caching initiatives.

Rule 20—Leverage Content Delivery Networks

> ### Rule 20: What, When, How, and Why
>
> **What:** Use CDNs (content delivery networks) to offload traffic
> from your site.
>
> **When to use:** Ensure it is cost justified and then choose which
> content is most suitable.
>
> **How to use:** Most CDNs leverage DNS (Domain Name Services
> or Domain Name Servers) to serve content on your site's behalf.
>
> **Why:** CDNs help offload traffic spikes and are often economical
> ways to scale parts of a site's traffic.
>
> **Key takeaways:** CDNs are a fast and simple way to offset spiki-
> ness of traffic as well as traffic growth in general. Make sure you
> perform a cost-benefit analysis and monitor the CDN usage.

The easiest way to handle a huge amount of user traffic is to
avoid it. Now there are two ways in which you can do this. The
first is by failing to scale, and having your site crash and all the
users leave. A better way to avoid the traffic is to get someone
else to handle as many of the requests as possible. This is where
the content delivery networks (CDNs) come in.

CDNs are a collection of computers, called *nodes* or *edge
servers*, connected via a network, called a *backbone*, that have
duplicate copies of their customers' data or content (images,
Web pages, and so on) on them. By strategically placing edge

servers on different Tier 1 networks and employing a myriad of
technologies and algorithms the CDN can direct requests to
nodes that are optimally suited to respond. This optimization
could be based on such things as the fewest network hops, highest availability, or fewest requests. The focus of this optimization
is most often the reduction of response times as perceived by the
end user, requesting person, or service.

How this works in practice can be demonstrated best by an
example, see Figure 6.1. Let's say the AKF blog was getting so
much traffic that we decided to employ a CDN. We would set
up a CNAME in DNS that pointed users requesting www.akf-
partners.com/techblog to 1107.c.cdn_vendor.net (see the DNS
table in Figure 6.1). The user's browser would then query DNS
for akfpartners.com (step 1), receive the CDN domain name
back (step 2), perform another DNS lookup on the CDN
domain (step 3), receive IPs associated with
1107.c.cdn_vendor.net (step 4), and route and receive the
request for our blog content to one of those IPs (steps 5-6). The
content of our blog would be cached on the CDN servers, and
periodically it would query the origin or originating server, in
this case our server hosting our blog, for updates.

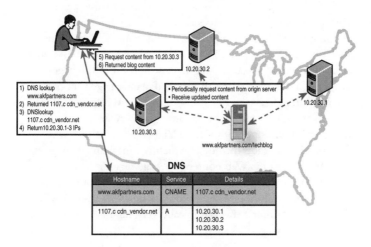

Figure 6.1   CDN example

As you can see in our example, the benefit of using a CDN in front of our own blog server is that the CDN takes all the requests (possibly hundreds or thousands per hour) and only requests from our server when checking for updated cache. This requires you to purchase fewer servers, less power, and smaller amounts of bandwidth, as well as fewer people required to maintain that infrastructure. This aid in scale, availability, and response time isn't free—it typically comes at a premium to your public peering (Internet peering) traffic costs. Often CDN providers price on either the 95th percentile of peak traffic (like many transit providers) or total traffic delivered. Rates drop on a per traffic delivered basis as the traffic increases. As a result, the analysis of when to convert to a CDN almost never works on a cost-only basis. You need to factor in the reduction in response time to end users, the likely resulting increase in user activity (faster response often elicits more transactions), the increase in availability of your site, and the reduction in server, power, and associated infrastructure costs. In most cases, we've found that clients with greater than 10M of avenue revenues are better served by implementing CDNs than continuing to serve that traffic themselves.

You might be thinking that all this caching sounds great for static Web sites but how does this help your dynamic pages? To start with even dynamic pages have static content. Images, JavaScript, CSS, and so on, are all usually static, which means they can be cached in a CDN. The actual text or content generated dynamically is usually the smallest portion of the page. Second, CDNs are starting to enable dynamic page support. Akamai offers a service called Dynamic Site Accelerator[1] that is used to accelerate and cache dynamic pages. Akamai was one of the companies, along with Oracle, Vignette, and others, who developed Edge Side Includes,[2] which is a markup language for assembling dynamic Web content on edge servers.

Whether you have dynamic or static pages on your site, consider adding a CDN into the mix of caches. This layer provides the benefit of faster delivery, typically very high availability, and less traffic on your site's servers.

Rule 21—Use Expires Headers

Rule 21: What, When, How, and Why

What: Use `Expires` headers to reduce requests and improve the scalability and performance of your system.

When to use: All object types need to be considered.

How to use: Headers can be set on Web servers or through application code.

Why: The reduction of object requests increases the page performance for the user and decreases the number of requests your system must handle per user.

Key takeaways: For each object type (IMAGE, HTML, CSS, PHP, and so on) consider how long the object can be cached for and implement the appropriate header for that timeframe.

It is a common misconception that pages can control how they are cached by placing meta tags, such as `Pragma`, `Expires`, or `Cache-Control`, in the `<HEAD>` element of the page. See the following code for examples. Unfortunately, meta tags in HTML are recommendations of how a page should be treated by the browser, but many browsers do not pay attention to these tags. Even worse, because proxy caches don't inspect the HTML, they do not abide by these tags at all.

```
<META HTTP-EQUIV="EXPIRES" CONTENT="Mon, 22 Aug 2011
11:12:01 GMT">
<META HTTP-EQUIV="Cache-Control" CONTENT="NO-CACHE">
```

HTTP headers, unlike meta tags, provide much more control over caching. This is especially true with regard to proxy caches because they do pay attention to headers. These headers cannot be seen in the HTML and are generated dynamically by the Web server or the code that builds the page. You can control them by configurations on the server or in code. A typical HTTP response header could look like this:

```
HTTP Status Code: HTTP/1.1 200 OK
Date: Thu, 21 Oct 2010 20:03:38 GMT
Server: Apache/2.2.9 (Fedora)
```

```
X-Powered-By: PHP/5.2.6
Expires: Mon, 26 Jul 2011 05:00:00 GMT
Last-Modified: Thu, 21 Oct 2010 20:03:38 GMT
Cache-Control: no-cache
Vary: Accept-Encoding, User-Agent
Transfer-Encoding: chunked
Content-Type: text/html; charset=UTF-8
```

A couple of the most pertinent headers for caching are the
`Expires` and `Cache-Control`. The `Expires` entity-header field
provides the date and time after which the response is considered stale. To mark a response as "never expires," the origin server should send a date one year from the time of response. In the
preceding example, notice the `Expires` header identifies the
date 26 July 2011 with a time of 05:00 GMT. If today's date was
26 June 2011, then the page requested would expire in approxi-
mately one month and should be refreshed from the server at
that time.

The `Cache-Control` general-header field is used to specify
directives that, in accordance with the Request For Comments
(RFC) 2616 Section 14 defining the HTTP 1.1 protocol, must
be obeyed by all caching mechanisms along the request/response
chain.[3] There are many directives that can be issued under the
header, including `public`, `private`, `no-cache`, and `max-age`. If
a response includes both an `Expires` header and a max-age
directive, the max-age directive overrides the `Expires` header,
even if the `Expires` header is more restrictive. Following are the
definitions of a few of the `Cache-Control` directives:

- `public`—The response may be cached by any cache,
  shared or nonshared.

- `private`—The response message is intended for a single
  user and must not be cached by a shared cache.

- `no-cache`—A cache must not use the response to satisfy a
  subsequent request without revalidation with the origin
  server.

- `max-age`—The response is stale if its current age is greater
  than the value given (in seconds) at the time of a request.

There are several ways to set HTTP headers, including through a Web server and through code. In Apache 2.2 the configurations are set in the httpd.conf file. `Expires` headers require the `mod_expires` module to be added to Apache.[4] There are three basic directives for the expires module. The first tells the server to activate the module, `ExpiresActive`. The next directive is to set the `Expires` header for a specific type of object such as images or text, `ExpiresByType`. The last directive is a default for how to handle all objects not specified by a type, `ExpiresDefault`. See the following code for an example:

```
ExpiresActive On
ExpiresByType image/png "access plus 1 day"
ExpiresByType image/gif "modification plus 5 hours"
ExpiresByType text/html "access plus 1 month 15 days 2 hours"
ExpiresDefault "access plus 1 month"
```

The other way to set HTTP `Expires` as well as `Cache-Control` and other headers is in code. In PHP this is pretty straightforward by using the `header()` command to send a raw HTTP header. This `header()` command must be called before any output is sent, either by HTML tags or from PHP. See the following sample PHP code for setting headers. Other languages have similar methods of setting headers.

```
<?php
header("Expires: 0");
header("Last-Modified: " . gmdate("D, d M Y H:i:s") . " GMT");
header("cache-control: no-store, no-cache, must-revalidate");
header("Pragma: no-cache");
?>
```

The last topic for this rule actually has nothing to do with headers but has to deal with configuring Web servers for optimization of performance and scale, so this is a good place to talk about it. *Keep-alives*, or HTTP persistent connections, allow for the reuse of TCP connections for multiple HTTP requests. In HTTP/1.1 all connections are considered persistent, and most Web servers default to allow keep-alives. According to the

Apache documentation the use of keep-alives has resulted in a
50% reduction in latency for HTML pages.[5] The default setting
in Apache's httpd.conf file is `KeepAlive On`, but the default
`KeepAliveTimeOut` is set at only 5 seconds. The benefit of
longer timeout periods is that more HTTP requests do not have
to establish, use, and break down TCP connections, but the benefit of short timeout periods is that the Web server threads will
not be tied up for servicing other requests. A balance between
the two based on the specifics of your application or site is
important.

As a practical example, we ran a test on one of our sites using
webpagetest.org, the open-source tool developed by AOL for
testing Web pages. The configuration was a simple MediaWiki
running on an Apache HTTP Server v 2.2. In Figure 6.2, the
results from the test on the wiki page with the keep-alives
turned off and the `Expires` headers not set are shown. The
initial page load was 3.8 seconds, and the repeat view as 2.3
seconds.

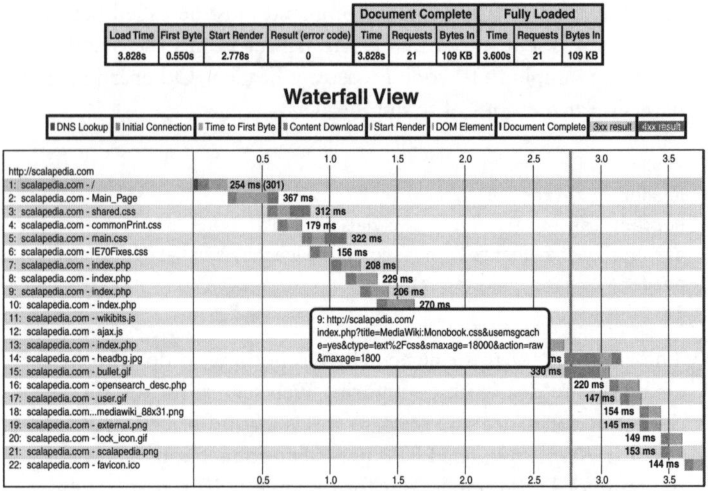

				Document Complete			Fully Loaded		
Load Time	First Byte	Start Render	Result (error code)	Time	Requests	Bytes In	Time	Requests	Bytes In
3.828s	0.550s	2.778s	0	3.828s	21	109 KB	3.600s	21	109 KB

Figure 6.2   Wiki page test (keep-alives off and
no `Expires` headers)

In Figure 6.3, the results are shown from the test on the wiki page with the keep-alives turned on and the `Expires` headers set. The initial page load was 2.6 seconds, and the repeat view as 1.4 seconds. This is a reduction in page load time of 32% for the initial page load and 37% for the repeat page load.

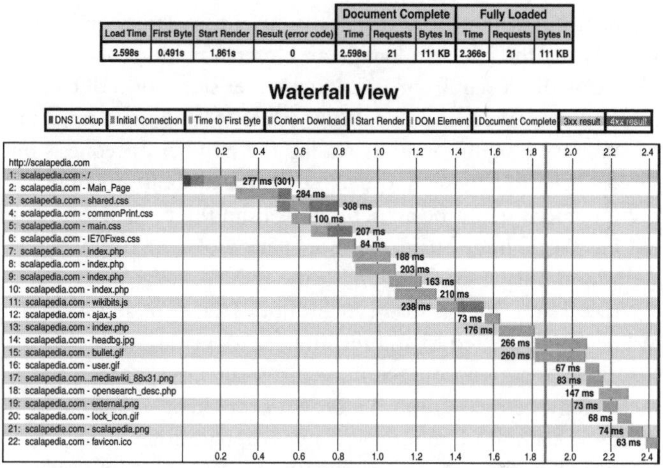

				Document Complete			Fully Loaded		
Load Time	First Byte	Start Render	Result (error code)	Time	Requests	Bytes In	Time	Requests	Bytes In
2.598s	0.491s	1.861s	0	2.598s	21	111 KB	2.366s	21	111 KB

Waterfall View

| ■ DNS Lookup | ■ Initial Connection | ■ Time to First Byte | ■ Content Download | ▮ Start Render | ▮ DOM Element | ▮ Document Complete | 3xx result | 4xx result |

Figure 6.3   Wiki page test (keep-alives on and `Expires` headers set)

Rule 22—Cache Ajax Calls

Rule 22: What, When, How, and Why

What: Use appropriate HTTP response headers to ensure cacheability of Ajax calls.

When to use: Every Ajax call but those absolutely requiring real time data that are likely to have been recently updated.

How to use: Modify `Last-Modified`, `Cache-Control`, and `Expires` headers appropriately.

Why: Decrease user perceived response time, increase user satisfaction, and increase the scalability of your platform or solution.

Key takeaways: Leverage Ajax and cache Ajax calls as much as possible to increase user satisfaction and increase scalability.

For newcomers or those unfamiliar with some fairly common Internet terms, think of Ajax as one of the "approaches" behind some of those drop-down menus that start to offer suggestions as you type, or the map services that allow you to zoom in and out of maps without making additional round-trip calls to a distant server. If handled properly, Ajax not only makes for wonderfully interactive user interfaces, it helps us in our scalability endeavors by allowing the client to handle and interact with data and objects without requiring additional server side work. But if not handled properly, Ajax can actually create some unique scalability constraints by significantly increasing the number of requests our servers need to handle. And make no mistake about it, while these requests might be asynchronous from the perspective of the browser, a huge burst in a short period of time may very well flood our server farms and cause them to fail.

Ajax is an acronym for Asynchronous JavaScript and XML. While often referred to as a technology, it's perhaps best described as a group of techniques, languages, approaches, and technologies employed on the browser (or client side) to help create richer and more interactive Web applications. While the items within this acronym are descriptive of many Ajax implementations, the actual interactions need not be asynchronous and need not make use of XML only as a data interchange format. JSON may take the place of XML for instance. JavaScript, however, is almost always used.

Jesse James Garrett is widely cited as coining the term Ajax in 2005 in his article "Ajax: A New Approach to Web Applications."[6] In a loose sense of the term, Ajax consists of standards-based presentation leveraging CSS and DHTML, interaction and dynamic display capabilities facilitated by the Document Object Model (or DOM), a data interchange and manipulation mechanism such as XML with XSLT or JSON, and a data retrieval mechanism. Data retrieval is often (but not absolutely necessarily) asynchronous from the end user perspective. JavaScript is the language used to allow everything to interact within the client browser. When asynchronous data transfer is used, the XMLHttpRequest object is used. The purpose of Ajax is to put an end to the herky-jerky interactions described by our first experiences with the Internet, where everything was a request and reply interaction. With this background behind us, we move on to some of the scalability concerns associated with Ajax and finally discuss how our friend caching might help us solve some of these concerns.

Clearly we all strive to create interfaces that increase user interaction and satisfaction and hopefully in so doing increase revenues, profits, and stakeholder wealth. Ajax is one method by which we might help facilitate a richer and more real time experience for our end users. Because it can help eliminate what would otherwise be unnecessary round-trips for interactions within our browser, user interactions can happen more quickly. Users can zoom in or zoom out without waiting for server responses, drop-down menus can be prepopulated based on previous entries, and users typing query strings into search bars can start to see potential search strings in which they might be interested to better guide their exploration. The asynchronous nature of Ajax can also help us load mail results into a client browser by repetitively fetching mail upon certain user actions without requiring the user to hit a "next page" button.

But some of these actions can also be detrimental to cost-effective scale of our platforms. Let's take the case of a user entering a search term for a specific product on a Web site. We may want to query a product catalog to populate suggested search terms for a user as he types in search terms. Ajax could help with such an implementation by using each successive keystroke to send a request to our servers, return a result based on what was typed thus far, and populate that result in a drop-down menu without a browser refresh as the user types. Or the returned result may be the full search results of an as yet uncompleted string as the user types! Examples of both implementations can be found in many search engines and commerce sites today. But allowing each successive keystroke to ultimately result in a search query to a server is both costly for our backend systems and might be wasteful. A user typing "beanie baby" for instance may cause 11 successive searches to be performed where only one is absolutely necessary. The user experience might be fantastic, but if the user types quickly as many as 8 to 10 of those searches may never actually return results before he finishes typing.

There is another way to achieve your goals without a 10x increase in traffic while achieving the same result and as you might expect given the theme of this chapter; it involves caching. With a little work, we can cache the results of previous Ajax interactions within the client browser and potentially within our CDNs (Rule 20), page caches (Rule 23), and application caches (Rule 24). Let's first look at how we can make sure that we leverage the cache in the browser.

Three key elements in ensuring that we can cache our content in the browser are the `Cache-Control` header, the `Expires` header, and the `Last-Modified` header of our HTTP response. Two of these we discussed in detail in Rule 21. For `Cache-Control` we want to avoid the `no-store` option and where possible we want to set the header to `public` so that any proxies and caches (such as a CDN) in between our end points (clients) and our servers can store result sets and serve them up to other requests. Of course we don't want private data set to public, but where possible we certainly want to leverage the high degree of caching that "public" offers us.

Remember that our goal is to eliminate round-trips to both decrease user perceived response time and decrease server load. As such, the `Expires` header of our response should be set far enough out into the future that the browser will cache the first result locally and read from it with subsequent requests. For static or semistatic objects, such as profile images or company logos, this might be set days or more out into the future. Some objects might have greater temporal sensitivity, such as the reading of a feed of friends' status updates. In these cases, we might set `Expires` headers out by seconds or maybe even minutes to both give the sense of real time behavior while reducing overall load.

The `Last-Modified` header helps us handle conditional GET requests. In these cases, consistent with the HTTP 1.1 protocol, the server should respond with a 304 status if the item in cache is appropriate or still valid. The key to all these points is, as the "Http" portion of the name XMLHttpRequest implies, that Ajax requests behave (or should behave) the same as any other HTTP request and response. Using our knowledge of these requests will aid us in ensuring that we increase the cacheability, usability, and scalability of all the systems that enable these requests.

While the previous approaches will help when we have content that we can modify in the browser, the problem becomes a bit more difficult when we use expanding search strings such as those we might find when a user interacts with a search page and starts typing a search string. There simply is no simple solution to this particular problem. But using `public` as the argument in the `Cache-Control` header will help to ensure that all similar search strings are cached in intermediate caches and proxies. Therefore common beginnings of search strings and common intermediate search strings have a good chance of being cached somewhere before we get them. This particular problem can be generalized to other specific objects within a page leveraging Ajax. For instance, systems that request specific objects such as an item for sale in an auction, a message in a social networking site, or an e-mail system should use specific message IDs rather than relative offsets when making requests. Relative names such as "page=3&item=2" that identify the second message in the third page of a system can change and cause coherency and consistency problems. Better terms would be "id=124556", with this ID representing an atomic item that does not change and can be cached for this user or future users where the item is public.

Easier to solve are the cases where we know that we have a somewhat static set or even semidynamic set of items such as a limited or context-sensitive product catalog. We can fetch these results, asynchronously from the client perspective, and both cache them for later use by the same client or perhaps more importantly ensure they are cached by CDNs and intermediate caches or proxies for other clients performing similar searches.

We close this rule by giving an example of a bad response to an Ajax call and a good response. The bad response may look like this:

```
HTTP Status Code: HTTP/1.1 200 OK
Date: Thu, 21 Oct 2010 20:03:38 GMT
Server: Apache/2.2.9 (Fedora)
X-Powered-By: PHP/5.2.6
Expires: Mon, 26 Jul 1997 05:00:00 GMT
Last-Modified: Thu, 21 Oct 2010 20:03:38 GMT
Pragma: no-cache
```

```
Vary: Accept-Encoding,User-Agent
Transfer-Encoding: chunked
Content-Type: text/html; charset=UTF-8
```

Using our three topics, we notice that our `Expires` header occurs in the past. We are missing the `Cache-Control` header completely, and the last modified header is consistent with the date that the response was sent; together, these force all GETs to grab new content. A more easily cached Ajax result would look like this:

```
HTTP Status Code: HTTP/1.1 200 OK
Date: Thu, 21 Oct 2010 20:03:38 GMT
Server: Apache/2.2.9 (Fedora)
X-Powered-By: PHP/5.2.6
Expires: Sun, 26 Jul 2020 05:00:00 GMT
Last-Modified: Thu, 31 Dec 1970 20:03:38 GMT
Cache-Control: public
Pragma: no-cache
Vary: Accept-Encoding,User-Agent
Transfer-Encoding: chunked
Content-Type: text/html; charset=UTF-8
```

In this example, we set the `Expires` header out to be well into the future, set the `Last-Modified` header to be well into the past, and told intermediate proxies that they can cache and reuse the object for other systems through `Cache-Control: public`.

Rule 23—Leverage Page Caches

Rule 23: What, When, How, and Why

What: Deploy page caches in front of your Web services.

When to use: Always.

How to use: Choose a caching system and deploy.

Why: Decrease load on Web servers by caching and delivering previously generated dynamic requests and quickly answering calls for static objects.

Key Takeaways: Page caches are a great way to offload dynamic requests and to scale cost effectively.

A *page cache* is a caching server you install in front of your Web servers to offload requests for both static and dynamic objects from those servers. Other common names for such a system or server are reverse proxy cache, reverse proxy server, and reverse proxy. We use the term page cache deliberately, because whereas a proxy might also be responsible for load balancing or SSL acceleration, we are simply focused on the impact that these caching servers have on our scalability. When implemented, the proxy cache looks like Figure 6.4.

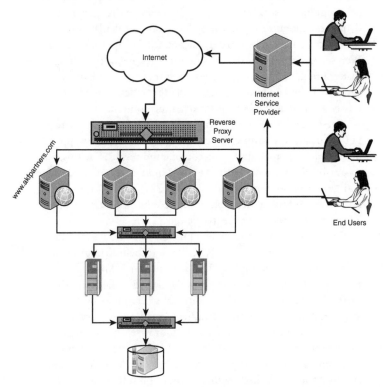

Figure 6.4   Proxy cache

Page caches handle some or all the requests until the pages or data that are stored in them is out of date or until the server receives a request for which it does not have the data. A failed request is known as a *cache miss* and might be a result of either a full cache with no room for the most recent request or an incompletely filled cache having either a low rate of requests or a recent restart. The cache miss is passed along to the Web server, which answers and populates the cache with the request, either replacing the least recently used record or taking up an unoccupied space.

There are three key arguments that we make in this rule. The first is that you should implement a page (or reverse proxy) cache in front of your Web servers and that in doing so you will get a significant scalability benefit. Web servers that generate dynamic content do significantly less work as calculated results (or responses) are appropriately cached for the appropriate time. Web servers that serve static content do not need to look up that content, and you can use fewer of them. We will, however, agree that the benefit of a page cache for static content isn't nearly as great as the benefit for dynamic content.

The second point is that you need to use the appropriate HTTP headers to ensure the greatest (but also business appropriate) cache potential of your content and results. For this, refer to our brief discussion of the `Cache-Control`, `Last-Modified`, and `Expires` headers in Rules 21 and 22. Section 14 of RFC 2616 has a complete description of these headers, their associated arguments, and the expected results.[7]

Our third point is that where possible you should include another HTTP header from RFC 2616 to help maximize the cacheability of your content. This new header is known as the `ETag`. The `ETag`, or entity tag, was developed to facilitate the method of If-None-Match conditional get requests by clients of a server. `ETags` are unique identifiers issued by the server for an object at the time of first request by a browser. If the resource on the server side is changed, a new `ETag` is assigned to it. Assuming appropriate support by the browser (client), the object and its `ETag` are cached by the browser and subsequent `If-None-Match` requests by the browser to the Web server will include the tag. If the tag matches, the server may respond with an HTTP 304 Not Modified response. If the tag is inconsistent with that on the server, the server will issue the updated object and its associated `ETag`.

The use of an `ETag` is optional, but to help ensure greater cacheability within page caches as well as all other proxy caches throughout the network transit of any given page or object, we highly recommend their use.

Rule 24—Utilize Application Caches

Rule 24: What, When, How, and Why

What: Alleviate temporal constraints in your system whenever possible.

When to use: Any time you are considering adding a constraint that an item or object maintains a certain state between a user's actions.

How to use: Relax constraints in the business rules.

Why: The difficulty in scaling systems with temporal constraints is significant because of the ACID properties (see definition in Chapter 2, "Distribute Your Work") of most RDBMSs (Relational Database Management Systems).

Key takeaways: Carefully consider the need for constraints such as items being available from the time a user views it until they purchase. Some possible edge cases where users are disappointed are much easier to compensate for than not being able to scale.

This isn't a section on how to develop an application cache. That's a topic for which you can get incredible, and free, advice by performing a simple search on your favorite Internet search engine. Rather we are going to make two basic but important points:

- The first is that you absolutely must employ application level caching if you want to scale in a cost-effective manner.

- The second is that such caching must be developed from a systems architecture perspective to effective long term.

We'll take it for granted that you agree wholeheartedly with our first point and spend the rest of this rule on our second point.

In both Rule 8 and Rule 9 (see Chapter 2), we hinted that the splitting of a platform (or an architecture) functionally by service or resource (Y Axis—Rule 8), or by something you knew about the requester or customer (Z Axis—Rule 9), could pay huge dividends in the cacheability of data to service requests. The question is which axis or rule to employ to gain what amount of benefit. The answer to that question likely changes over time as you develop new features or functions with new data requirements. The implementation approach, then, needs to change over time to accommodate the changing needs of your business. The process to identify these changing needs, however, remains the same. The learning organization needs to constantly analyze production traffic, costs per transaction, and user perceived response times to identify early indications of bottlenecks as they arise within the production environment and feed that data into the architecture team responsible for making changes.

The key question to answer here is what type of split, or refinement of a split, will gain the greatest benefit from a scalability and cost perspective? It is entirely possible that through an appropriate split implementation, and with the resulting cacheability of data within the application servers, that 100 or even 100,000 servers can handle double, triple, or even 10x the current production traffic. To illustrate this, let's walk through a quick example of a common ecommerce site, a fairly typical SaaS site focused on servicing business needs and a social networking or social interaction site.

Our ecommerce site has a number of functions, including search, browse, image inspection (including zooming), account update, sign-in, shopping cart, checkout, suggested items, and so on. Analysis of current production traffic indicates that 80% of our transactions across many of our most heavily used functions, including searching, browsing, and suggested products, occur across less than 20% of our inventory. Here we can leverage the Pareto Principle and deploy a Y axis (functional) split for these types of services to leverage the combined high number of hits on a comparatively small number of objects by our entire user base. Cacheability will be high, and our dynamic systems can benefit from the results delivered pursuant to similar earlier requests.

We may also find out that we have a number of power users—users who are fairly frequent in their requests. For these user-specific functions, we can decide to employ a Z axis split for user-specific functionality such as sign-in, shopping cart, account update (or other account information), and so on. While we can probably hypothesize about these events, clearly it is valuable to get real production data from our existing revenue producing site to help inform our decisions.

As another example, let's imagine that we have a SaaS business that helps companies handle customer support operations through hosted phone services, e-mail services, chat services, and a relationship management system. In this system, there are a great number of rules unique to any given business. On a per-business basis, these rules might require a great deal of memory to cache the rules and data necessary for a number of business operations. If you've immediately jumped to the conclusion that a customer-oriented or Z axis split is the right approach you are correct. But we also want to maintain some semblance of multitenancy both within the database and the application. How do we accomplish this and still cache our heaviest users to scale cost-effectively? Our answer, again, is the Pareto Principle. We can take the 20% of our largest businesses that might represent 80% of our total transaction volumes (such a situation exists with most of our customers) and spread them across several swimlanes of database splits. To gain cost leverage, we take the 80% of our smaller users and sprinkle them evenly across all these swimlanes. The theory here is that the companies with light utilization are going to experience low cache hit rates even if they exist among themselves. As such, we might as well take our larger customers and allow them to benefit from caching while gaining cost leverage from our smaller customers. Those smaller customer experiences aren't going to be significantly different unless we host them on their own dedicated systems, which as we all know runs counter to the cost benefits we expect to receive in a SaaS environment.

Our last example deals with a social network or interaction site. As you might expect, we are again going to apply the Pareto Principle and information from our production environment to help guide our decisions. Social networks often involve a small number of users with an incredibly skewed percentage of traffic. Sometimes these users are active consumers, sometimes they are active producers (destinations where other people go), and sometimes they are both.

Our first step might be to identify whether there is a small percentage of information or subsites that have a disproportionately high percentage of the "read" traffic. Such nodes within our social network can help guide us in our architectural considerations and might lead us to perform Z axis splits for these producers such that their nodes of activity are highly cacheable from a read perspective. Assuming the Pareto Principle holds true (as it typically does), we've now serviced nearly 80% of our read traffic with a small number of servers (and potentially page/proxy caches—see Rule 23). Our shareholders are happy because we can service requests with very little capital intensity.

What about the very active producers of contents and/or updates within our social network? The answer may vary depending on whether their content also has a high rate of consumption (reads) or sits mostly dormant. In the case where these users have both high production (write/update) rates and high consumption (read) rates, we can just publish their content directly to the swimlane or node in which it is being read. If read and write conflicts start to become a concern as these "nodes" get hot, we can use read replication and horizontal scale techniques (the X axis or Rule 7), or we can start to think about how we order and asynchronously apply these updates over time (see Chapter 11, "Asynchronous Communication and Message Buses"). As we continue to grow, we can mix these techniques. If we still have troubles, after caching aggressively from the browser through CDNs to page and application caches (the rules in this chapter), we can continue to refine our splits. Maybe we enforce a hierarchy within a given user's updates and start to split them along content boundaries (another type of Y axis split—Rule 8), or perhaps we just continue to create read replicas of data instances (X axis—Rule 7). Maybe we identify that the information that is being read has a unique geographic bias as is the case with some types of news and we begin to split the data along geolocation determined boundaries by request, which is something we know about the requester and therefore another type of Z axis split (Rule 9).

With any luck, you've identified a pattern in this rule. The first step is to hypothesize as to likely usage and determine ways to split to maximize cacheability. After implementing these splits in both the application and supporting persistent data stores, evaluate their effectiveness in production. Further refine your approach based on production data and iteratively apply the Pareto Principle and the AKF Scale Cube (Rules 7, 8, and 9) to refine and increase cache hit rates. Lather, rinse, repeat.

Rule 25—Make Use of Object Caches

Rule 25: What, When, How, and Why

What: Implement object caches to help your system scale.

When to use: Any time you have repetitive queries or computations.

How to use: Select any one of the many open source or vendor supported solutions and implement the calls in your application code.

Why: A fairly straightforward object cache implementation can save a lot of computational resources on application servers or database servers.

Key takeaways: Consider implementing an object cache anywhere computations are performed repeatedly, but primarily this is done between the database and application tiers.

Object caches are simply in-process data stores (usually in memory) that store a hashed summary of each item. These caches are used primarily for caching data that may be computationally expensive to regenerate, such as the result set of complex database queries. A hash function is a mathematical function that converts a large and variable-sized amount of data, into a small hash value.[8] This hash value (also called a hash sum or checksum) is usually an integer that can be used as an index in an array. This is by no means a full explanation of hash algorithms as the design and implementation of them are a domain unto itself, but you can test several of these on Linux systems with `cksum`, `md5sum`, and `sha1sum` as shown in the following code. Notice how variable lengths of data result in consistent 128-bit hashes.

```
# echo 'AKF Partners' | md5sum
90c9e7fd09d67219b15e730402d092eb  -
# echo 'Hyper Growth Scalability AKF Partners' | md5sum
faa216d21d711b81dfcddf3631cbe1ef  -
```

There are many different varieties of object caches such as the popular Memcached, Apache's OJB, and NCache just to name a few. As varied as the choice of tools are the implementations. Object caches are most often implemented between the database and the application to cache result sets from SQL queries. However, some people use object caches for results of complex application computations such as user recommendations, product prioritization, or reordering advertisements based on recent past performance. The object cache in front of a database tier is the most popular implementation because often the database is the most difficult and most expensive to scale. If you have the ability to postpone the split of a database or the purchase of a larger server, which is *not* a recommended approach to scaling, by implementing an object cache this is an easy decision. Let's talk about how to decide when to pull the trigger and implement an object cache.

Besides the normal suspects of CPU and memory utilization by the database, one of the most telling pieces of data that indicates when your system is in need of an object cache is the Top SQL report. This is a generic name for any report or tool that is used to mean any report generated to show the most frequently and most resource-intensive queries run on the database. Oracle's Enterprise Manager Grid Control has a Top SQL Assessment built in for identifying the most resource intensive SQL statements. Besides using this data to identify and prioritize the improvement of slow running queries, this data can also be used to show which queries could be eliminated from the database by adding caching. There are equivalent reports or tools either built in or offered as add-ons for all the popular databases.

Once you've decided you need an implementation of an object cache, you then need to choose one that best fits your needs and implement it. A word of caution for those engineering teams that at this point might be considering building a home-grown solution. There are more than enough production-grade object cache solutions to choose from. As an example, Facebook uses more than 800 servers supplying more than 28 terabytes of memory for its system.[9] While there are possible reasons that might drive you to make a decision to build an object cache instead of buying/using an open source product this decision should be highly scrutinized.

The next step is to actually implement the object cache, which depending on the product selected is straightforward. Memcached supports clients for many different programming languages such as Java, Python, and PHP. In PHP the two primary commands are get and set. In the following example you can see that we connect to the memcached server. If that fails we just query the database through a function we call dbquery, not shown in the example. If the memcached connection succeeds we attempt to retrieve the $data that is associated with a particular $key. If that get fails, then we query the db and set the $data into memcached so that the next time we look for that data it is in memcached. The false flag in the set command is for compression and the 90 is for the expiration time in seconds.

```
$memcache = new Memcache;
If ($memcache->connect('127.0.0.1', 11211)) {
        If ($data = $memcache->get('$key')) {
     } else {
                $data = dbquery($key);
                $memcache->set('$key',$data, false, 90);
        }
} else {
        $data = dbquery($key);
}
```

The final step in implementing the object cache is to monitor it for the cache hit rate. This ratio is the number of times the system requests an object that is in the cache compared to the total number of requests. Ideally this ratio is 85% or better, meaning that the requests for objects is not in cache or expired in cache only 15% or less of the time. If the cache hit ratio drops, you need to consider adding more object cache servers.

Rule 26—Put Object Caches on Their Own "Tier"

Rule 26: What, When, How, and Why

What: Use a separate tier in your architecture for object caches.

When to use: Any time you have implemented object caches.

How to use: Move object caches onto their own servers.

Why: The benefits of a separate tier are better utilization of memory and CPU resources and having the ability to scale the object cache independently of other tiers.

Key takeaways: When implementing an object cache it is simplest to put the service on an existing tier such as the application servers. Consider implementing or moving the object cache to its own tier for better performance and scalability.

In Rule 25 we covered the basics of implementing an object cache. We left off with you monitoring the object cache for cache hit ratio and when this dropped below ~85% we suggested that you consider expanding the object cache pool. In this rule, we're going to discuss where to implement the object cache pool and whether it should reside on its own tier within your application architecture.

Many companies start with the object cache on the Web or application servers. This is a simple implementation that works well to get people up and running on an object cache without an investment in additional hardware or virtual instances if operating within a cloud. The downside to this is that the object cache takes up a lot of memory on the server, and it can't be scaled independently of the application or Web tier when needed.

A better alternative is to put the object cache on its own tier of servers. This would be between the application servers and the database, if using the object cache to cache query result sets. If caching objects created in the application tier, this object cache tier would reside between the Web and application servers. See Figure 6.5 for a diagram of what this architecture would look like. This is a logic architecture in that the object cache tier could be a single physical tier of servers that are used for both database object caching as well as application object caching.

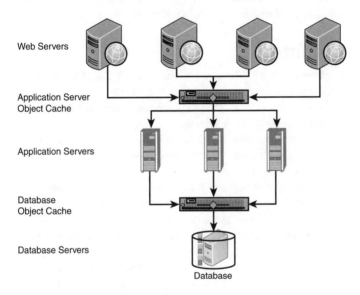

Figure 6.5   Object cache

The advantage of separating these tiers is that you can size the servers appropriately in terms of how much memory and CPU are required, and you can scale the number of servers in this pool independently of other pools. Sizing the server correctly can save quite a bit of money since object caches typically require a lot of memory—most all store the objects and keys in memory—but require relatively low computational processing power. You can also add servers as necessary and have all the additional capacity utilized by the object cache rather than splitting it with an application or Web service.

Summary

In this chapter, we offered seven rules for caching. We have so many rules dedicated to this one subject because there are a myriad of caching options to consider but also because caching is a proven way to scale a system. By caching at every level from the browser through the network all the way through your application to the databases, you can achieve significant improvements in performance as well as scalability.

Endnotes

1. Akamai Solution, "Dynamic Site Accelerator," 2008, http://www. akamai.com/dl/brochures/akamai_dsa_sb.pdf.

2. Mark Tsimelzon et al., W3C, "ESI Language Specification 1.0," http://www.w3.org/TR/esi-lang.

3. R. Fielding et al., Networking Group Request for Comments 2616, June 1999, "Hypertext Transfer Protocol—HTTP/1.1," http://www. ietf.org/rfc/rfc2616.txt.

4. Apache HTTP Server Version 2.0, "Apache Module mod_expires," http://httpd.apache.org/docs/2.0/mod/mod_expires.html.

5. Apache HTTP Server Version 2.0, Apache Core Features, "KeepAlive Directive," http://httpd.apache.org/docs/current/mod/core.html# keepalive.

6. Jesse James Garrett, "Ajax: A New Approach to Web Applications," Adaptive Path.com, "Ideas: Essays and Newsletter," February 18, 2005, http://www.adaptivepath.com/ideas/essays/archives/ 000385.php.

7. Fielding et al., Hypertext Transfer Protocol/1.1, "Header Field Definitions," http://www.w3.org/Protocols/rfc2616/rfc2616-sec14. html.

8. Wikipedia, "Hash function," http://en.wikipedia.org/wiki/ Hash_function.

9. Paul Saab, "Scaling memcached at Facebook," December 12, 2008, http://www.facebook.com/note.php?note_id=39391378919& ref=mf.

7

Learn from Your Mistakes

Research has long supported the position that we learn more from our failures than from our successes. But we can only truly learn from our failures if we foster an environment of open, honest communication and fold in lightweight processes that help us repeatedly learn and get the most from our mistakes and failures. Rather than emulate the world of politics, where failures are hidden from others and as a result bound to be repeated over time, we should strive to create an environment in which we share our failures as antipatterns to best practices. To be successful, we need to learn aggressively, rely on organizations like Quality Assurance (QA) appropriately, expect systems to fail, and design for those failures appropriately and treat each failure as a precious learning opportunity.

Rule 27—Learn Aggressively

> **Rule 27: What, When, How, and Why**
>
> **What:** Take every opportunity to learn.
>
> **When to use:** Be constantly learning from your mistakes as well as successes.
>
> **How to use:** Watch your customers or use A/B testing to determine what works. Use postmortems to learn from incidents and problems in production.

> **Why:** Doing something without measuring the results or having an incident without learning from it are wasted opportunities that your competitors are taking advantage of.
>
> **Key takeaways:** Be constantly and aggressively learning. The companies that learn best, fastest, and most often are the ones that grow the fastest and are the most scalable.

Do people in your organization think they know everything there is to know about building great, scalable products? Or perhaps your organization thinks it knows better than the customer. Have you heard someone say that customers don't know what they want? Although it might be true that customers can't necessarily articulate what they want, that doesn't mean they don't know it when they see it. Failing to learn continuously and aggressively, meaning at every opportunity, will leave you vulnerable to competitors who are willing to constantly learn.

Our continuing research on social contagion (also known as viral growth) of Internet-based products and services has revealed that organizations that possess a learning culture are far more likely to achieve viral growth than those that do not. In case you're not familiar with the terms *social contagion* or *viral growth*, the term *viral* derives from epidemiology (the study of health and illness in populations) and is used in reference to Internet-based companies to explain how things spread from user to user. The exponential growth of users is known as viral growth and implies the intentional sharing of information by people. In nature most people do not intentionally spread viruses, but on the Internet they do in the form of information or entertainment, and the resulting spread is similar to a virus. Once this exponential growth starts it is possible to accurately predict its rate because it follows a power law distribution until the product reaches a point of nondisplacement. Figure 7.1 shows the growth in cumulative users for a product achieving viral growth (solid line) and one that just barely misses the tipping point by less than 10%.

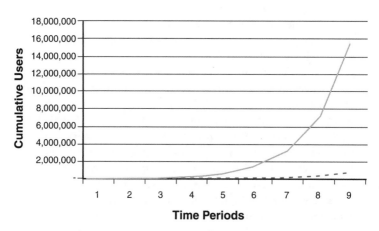

Figure 7.1   Viral growth

The importance of creating a culture of learning cannot be underestimated. Even if you're not interested in achieving viral growth but want to produce great products for your customers, you must be willing to learn. There are two areas in which learning is critical. The first, as we have been discussing, is from the customers. The second is from the operations of the business/technology. We discuss each briefly in turn. Both rely on excellent listening skills. We believe that we were given two ears and one mouth to remind us to listen more than we talk.

Focus groups are interesting because you get an opportunity to sit down with your customers and hear what they think. The problem is that they, like most of us, can't really know how they will react to a product until they get to see and feel it in their own living room/computer. Not to delve too deeply into the philosophical realm, but this in part is caused by what is known as *social construction*. Put very simply, we make meaning of everything (and we do mean everything—it's been argued that we do this for reality itself) by labeling things with the meaning that is most broadly held within our social groups. While we can form our own opinions, they are most often just reflections or built on what others believe. So, how do you get around this problem of not being able to trust what customers say? Launch quickly and watch your customers' reactions.

Watching your customers can be done in a number of ways. Simply keeping track of usage and adoption of new features is a great start. The more classic A/B testing is even better. This is when you segment your customers into A-group and B-group randomly and allow A-group to have access to one version of the product and B-group to the other version. By comparing results, such as abandonment rates, time spent on site, conversion rates, and so on you can decide which version performs better. Obviously some forethought must be put into the metrics that are going to be measured, but this is a great and fairly accurate way to compare product versions.

The other areas in which you must constantly learn if you want to achieve scalability are technology and business operations. We'll talk more about this topic in Rule 30, but you must not let incidents or problems pass without learning from them. Every site issue, outage, or downtime is an opportunity to learn how to do things better in the future. If you don't take time to perform a postmortem on the incident, get to the *real* root cause, and put that learning back into the organization so that you don't have that same failure again, then you are bound to repeat your failures. Our philosophy is that while mistakes are unavoidable, making the same mistake twice is unacceptable. If a poor performing query doesn't get caught until it goes into production and results in a site outage, then we must get to the real root cause and fix it. In this case the root cause goes beyond the poorly performing query and includes the process and people that allowed it to get to production. By establishing a peer review of all code, DBA review of all queries, or even a load and performance test, we can minimize the chance that we allow poor performing queries into our production environment. The key here is to learn from everything—mistakes as well as successes.

Rule 28—Don't Rely on QA to Find Mistakes

Rule 28: What, When, How, and Why

What: Use QA to lower the cost of delivered products, increase engineering throughput, identify quality trends, and decrease defects—*not* to increase quality.

When to use: Whenever you can get greater throughput by hiring someone focused on testing rather than writing code. Use QA to learn from past mistakes—always.

How to use: Hire a QA person anytime you get greater than one engineer's worth of output with the hiring of a single QA person.

Why: Reduce cost, increase delivery volume/velocity, decrease the number of repeated defects.

Key takeaways: QA doesn't increase the quality of your system, as you can't test quality into a system. If used properly, it can increase your productivity while decreasing cost and most importantly it can keep you from increasing defect rates faster than your rate of organization growth during periods of rapid hiring.

Rule 28 has an ugly and slightly misleading and controversial title meant to provoke thought and discussion. Of course it makes sense to have a team responsible for testing products to identify defects. The issue is that you shouldn't rely solely on these teams to identify all your defects anymore than airlines rely on flight attendants for safe landings of their planes. At the heart of this view is one simple fact: You can't test quality into your system. Testing only identifies issues that you created during development, and as a result it is an identification of value that you destroyed and can recapture. Testing typically only finds mistakes, which often requires rework that in turn increases the marginal cost per unit of work (functionality) delivered. It is rare that testing, or the group that performs it, identifies untapped opportunities that might create additional value.

Don't get us wrong—QA definitely has an important role in an engineering organization. It is a role that is even more important when companies are growing at an incredibly fast rate and needing to scale their systems. The primary role of QA is to help identify product problems at a lower cost than having engineers perform the same task. Two important derived benefits from this role are to increase engineering velocity and to increase the rate of defect detection.

These benefits are achieved similarly to the fashion in which the industrial revolution reduced the cost of manufacturing and increased the number of units produced. By pipelining the process of engineering and allowing engineers to focus primarily on building products (and of course unit testing them), less time is spent per engineer in the setup and teardown of the testing process. Engineers now have more time per day to focus on building applications for the business. Typically we see both output per hour and output per day increase as a result of this. Cost per unit drops as a result of higher velocity at static cost. Additionally, the headcount cost of a great QA organization typically is lower on a per-head basis than the cost of an engineering organization, which further reduces cost. Finally, as the testing organization is focused and incented to identify defects, they don't have any psychological conflicts with finding problems within their own code (as many engineers do) or the code of a good engineering friend who sits next to them.

When to Hire a QA Person

You should hire a QA person anytime you can get one or more engineer's worth of productivity out of hiring someone in QA. The math is fairly simple. If you have 11 engineers, and each of them spends roughly 10% of her time on testing activities that could be done by a single QA person, then by hiring that QA person you can get 1.1 engineer's worth of productivity back by hiring a single QA person. Typically that person will also come at lower cost than an engineer, so you get 1.1 engineer's worth of work at .8 or .9 the cost of an engineer.

None of this argues against pairing engineers and QA personnel together as in the case of well run Agile processes. In fact, for many implementations, we recommend such an approach. But the division of labor is still valuable and typically achieves the goals of reducing cost, increasing defect identification, and increasing throughput.

But the greatest as of yet unstated value of QA organizations arises in the case of hyper growth companies. It's not that this value doesn't exist within static companies or companies of lower growth, but it becomes even more important in situations where engineering organizations are doubling (or more) in size annually. In these situations, standards are hard to enforce. Engineers with greater tenure within the organization simply don't have time to keep up with and enforce existing standards and even less time to identify the need for new standards that address scale, quality, or availability needs. In the case where a team doubles year over year, beginning year three of the doubling, half of the existing "experienced" team only has a year or less of company experience!

That brings us to why this rule is in the chapter on learning from mistakes. Imagine an environment in which managers spend nearly half of their time interviewing and hiring engineers and in which in any given year half of the engineers (or more) have less than a full year with the company. Imagine how much time the existing longer tenured engineers will be spending trying to teach the newer engineers about the source code management system, the build environments, the production environments, and so on. In such an environment too little time is spent validating that things have been built correctly, and the number of mistakes released into QA (but hopefully not production) increases significantly.

In these environments, it is QA's job to teach the organization what is happening from a quality perspective and where it is happening such that the engineering organization can adapt and learn. QA then becomes a tool to help the organization learn what mistakes it is making repeatedly, where those mistakes lie, and ideally how the organization can keep from making them in the future. QA is likely the only team capable of seeing the recurring problems.

Newer engineers, without the benefit of seeing their failures and the impacts of those failures, will likely not only continue to make them, but the approaches that lead to these failures will become habit. Worse yet, they will likely train those bad habits in the newly hired engineers as they arrive. What started out as a small increase in the rate of defects will become a vicious cycle.

Everyone will be running around attempting to identify the root cause of the quality nightmare, when the nightmare was bound to happen and is staring them in the face: a failure to learn from past mistakes!

QA must work to identify where a growing organization is having recurring problems and create an environment in which those problems are discussed and eliminated. And here, finally, is the most important benefit of QA—it helps an organization learn from engineering failures. Understanding that they can't test quality into the system, and unwilling to accept a role as a safety screen behind a catcher in baseball to stop uncaught balls, the excellent QA organization seeks to identify systemic failures in the engineering team that lead to later quality problems. This goes beyond the creation of burn down charts and find/fix ratios; it involves digging into and identifying themes of problems and their sources. Once these themes are identified, they are presented along with ideas on how to solve the problems.

Rule 29—Failing to Design for Rollback Is Designing for Failure

Rule 29: What, When, How, and Why

What: Always have the ability to roll back code.

When to use: Ensure all releases have the ability to roll back, practice it in a staging or QA environment, and use it in production when necessary to resolve customer incidents.

How to use: Clean up your code and follow a few simple procedures to ensure you can roll back your code.

Why: If you haven't experienced the pain of not being able to roll back, you likely will at some point if you keep playing with the "fix-forward" fire.

Key takeaways: Don't accept that the application is too complex or that you release code too often as excuses that you can't roll back. No sane pilot would take off in an airplane without the ability to land, and no sane engineer would roll code that they could not pull back off in an emergency.

To set the right mood for this next rule we should all be gathered around a campfire late at night telling scary stories. The story we're about to tell you is your classic scary story, including the people who hear scary noises in the house but don't get out. Those foolish people who ignored all the warning signs were us. As head of engineering and Chief Technology Officer (CTO), we believed and had been told by almost every manager, architect, and engineer that the application was too complex and not capable of being rolled back. We had several outages/issues after code releases that required a mad scramble to "fix-forward" and get a hot fix out later that same day to fully restore service. We lived with these minor inconveniences because we believed that the application was too complex to roll back.

Along came a major infrastructure release that, like all releases that came before, could not be rolled back. This release was the release-from-hell. Everything looked fine during the wee hours of the morning, but when traffic picked up as the East Coast woke up, the site went down. Had we been able to roll back, we could have done so at that point with a few upset customers and a bruised ego but nothing worse. But we couldn't. So we coddled the site all day adding capacity, throttling traffic, and so on, trying to keep things working until we had a fix. We pushed a patch late that evening and without the traffic on the site, thought we'd fixed it. The next morning, as traffic increased, the site started having problems again. This pattern of push a fix at night, without traffic think it's fixed, only to find out the next day that the site still had issues carried on for more than a week.

By the end of that week everyone was exhausted from being up literally days in a row. We finally pushed a patch that completely bypassed the original changes and were able to stabilize the site. While many lessons were learned from that incident, including failures of leadership, the one most relevant for this rule is that all that pain, to us as well as to our customers, could have been avoided had we been able to roll back the code.

One of the actions that came out of our postmortem was no more code was allowed to be released that couldn't be rolled back. At that point we had no choice but to make that edict, the business had zero tolerance for any more pain of that nature, and every single engineer understood that need as well. Six weeks later, when the next release was ready, we had the ability to roll back. What we all thought were insurmountable challenges turned out to be reasonably straightforward.

The following bulleted points provided us and many other teams since then the ability to roll back. As you'd expect the majority of the problem with rolling back is in the database. By going through the application to clean up any outstanding issues and then adhering to some simple rules every team should be able to roll back.

- **Database changes must only be additive**—Columns or tables should only be added, not deleted, until the next version of code is released that deprecates the dependency on those columns. Once these standards are implemented every release should have a portion dedicated to cleaning up the last release's data that is no longer needed.

- **DDL and DML scripted and tested**—The database changes that are to take place for the release must be scripted ahead of time instead of applied by hand. This should include the rollback script. The two reasons for this are that 1) the team needs to test the rollback process in QA or staging to validate that they have not missed something that would prevent rolling back and 2) the script needs to be tested under some amount of load condition to ensure it can be executed while the application is utilizing the database.

- **Restricted SQL queries in the application**—The development team needs to disambiguate all SQL by removing all SELECT * queries and adding column names to all UPDATE statements.

- **Semantic changes of data**—The development team must not change the definition of data within a release. An example would be a column in a ticket table that is currently being used as a status semaphore indicating three values such as assigned, fixed, or closed. The new version of the application cannot add a fourth status until code is first released to handle the new status and then code can be released to utilize the new status.

- **Wire On/Wire Off**—The application should have a framework added that allows code paths and features to be accessed by some users and not by others, based on an external configuration. This setting can be in a configuration file or a database table and should allow for both role-based access as well as random percentage based. This framework allows for beta testing of features with a limited set of users and allows for quick removal of a code path in the event of a major bug in the feature, without rolling back the entire code base.

We learned a painful but valuable lesson that left scars so deep we never pushed another piece of code that couldn't be rolled back. Even though we moved on to other positions with other teams, we carried that requirement with us. As you can see from the preceding guidelines these are not overly complex but rather straightforward rules that any team can apply and have rollback capability going forward.

Rule 30—Discuss and Learn from Failures

Rule 30: What, When, How, and Why

What: Leverage every failure to learn and teach important lessons.

When to use: Always.

How to use: Employ a postmortem process and hypothesize failures in low failure environments.

Why: We learn best from our mistakes—not our successes.

Key takeaways: Never let a good failure go to waste. Learn from every one and identify the technology, people, and process issues that need to be corrected.

Many of us, when discussing world events at social gatherings, have likely uttered sentences something to the effect of "We never seem to learn from history." But how many of us truly apply that standard to ourselves, our inventions, and our organizations within our work? There exists an interesting paradox within our world of highly available and highly scalable technology platforms: Those systems that are initially built the best fail less often and as a result the organizations have less opportunity to learn. Inherent to this paradox is the notion that each failure of process, systems, or people offers us an opportunity to perform a "postmortem" of the event for the purposes of learning and modifying our systems. A failure to leverage these precious events to improve our people, processes, and technology dooms us to continuing to operate exactly as we do today, which in turn means a failure to improve. A failure to improve, when drawn on a business contextual canvas of hyper growth and therefore a need for aggressive scale, becomes a painting depicting business failure. Too many things happen in our business when we are growing quickly to believe that a solution that we designed two years or even one year ago will be capable of supporting a business 10x the size of the time we built the system.

The world of nuclear power generation offers an interesting insight into this need to learn from our mistakes. In 1979, the TMI-2 reactor at Three Mile Island experienced a partial core meltdown, creating the most significant nuclear power accident in U.S. history. This accident became the source of several books, at least one movie, and two important theories on the source and need for learning in environments in which accidents are rare but costly.

Charles Perrow's Normal Accident Theory hypothesizes that the complexity inherent to modern coupled systems makes accidents inevitable.[1] The coupling inherent to these systems allows interactions to escalate rapidly with little opportunity for humans or control systems to interact successfully. Think back to how often you might have watched your monitoring solution go from all "green" to nearly completely red before you could respond to the first alert message.

Todd LaPorte, who developed the theory of High Reliability Organizations, believes that even in the case of an absence of accidents from which an organization can learn, there are organizational strategies to achieve higher reliability.[2] While the authors of these theories do not agree on whether these theories can coexist, they share certain common elements. The first is that organizations that fail often have greater opportunities to learn and grow than those that do not, assuming of course that they take an opportunity to learn from them. The second, which sort of follows from the first, is that systems that fail infrequently offer little opportunity to learn and as a result in the absence of other approaches the teams and systems will not grow and improve.

Having made the point that learning from and improving after mistakes is important, let's depart from that subject briefly to describe a lightweight process by which we can learn and improve. For any major issue that we experience, we believe an organization should attack that issue with a postmortem process that addresses the problem in three distinct but easily described phases:

- **Phase 1 Timeline**—Focus on generating a timeline of the events leading up to the issue or crisis. Nothing is discussed other than the timeline during this first phase. The phase is complete once everyone in the room agrees that there are no more items to be added to the timeline. We typically find that even after we've completed the timeline phase, people will continue to remember or identify timeline worthy events in the next phase of the postmortem.

- **Phase 2 Issue Identification**—The process facilitator walks through the timeline and works with the team to identify issues. Was it okay that the first monitor identified customer failures at 8 a.m. but that no one responded until noon? Why didn't the auto-failover of the database occur as expected? Why did we believe that dropping the user_authorization table would allow the application to start running again? Each and every issue is identified from the timeline, but no corrections or actions are allowed to be made until the team is done identifying issues. Invariably, team members will start to suggest actions, but it is the responsibility of the process facilitator to focus the team on issue identification during Phase 2.

- **Phase 3 State Actions**—Each item should have at least one action associated with it. The process facilitator walks down the list of issues and works with the team to identify an action, an owner, an expected result, and a time by which it should be completed. Using the SMART principles, each action should be specific, measurable, attainable, realistic, and timely. A single owner should be identified, even though the action may take a group or team to accomplish.

No postmortem should be considered complete until it has addressed the people, process, and technology issues responsible for the failure. Too often we find that clients stop at "a server died" as a root cause for an incident. Hardware fails, as do people and processes, and as a result no single failure should ever be considered the "true root cause" of any incident. The real question for any failure of scalability or availability is to ask "why didn't the holistic system act more appropriately?" If a database fails due to load, why didn't the organization identify the need earlier? What process or monitoring should have been in place to help the organization find the issue? Why did the failure take so long to recover? Why isn't the database split up such that any failure has less of an impact on our customer base or services? Why wasn't there a read replica that could be quickly promoted as the write database? In our experience, you are never finished unless you can answer "Why" at least five times to cover five different potential problems.

Now that we've discussed what we should do, let's return to the case where we don't have many opportunities to develop such a system. Weick and Sutcliffe have a solution for organizations lucky enough to have built platforms that scale effectively and fail infrequently.[3] Their solution, as modified to fit our needs, is described as follows:

- **Preoccupation with failure**—This practice is all about monitoring our product and our systems and reporting errors in a timely fashion. Success, they argue, narrows perceptions and breeds overconfidence. To combat the resulting complacency, organizations need complete transparency into system faults and failures. Reports should be widely distributed and discussed frequently such as in a daily meeting to discuss the operations of the platform.

- **Reluctance to simplify interpretations**—Take nothing for granted and seek input from diverse sources. Don't try to box failures into expected behavior and act with a healthy bit of paranoia. The human tendency here is to explain small variations as being "the norm," whereas they can easily be your best early indicator of future failure.

- **Sensitivity to operations**—Look at detail data at the minute level. Include the usage of real time data and make ongoing assessments and continual updates of this data.

- **Commitment to resilience**—Build excess capability by rotating positions and training your people in new skills. Former employees of eBay operations can attest that DBAs, SAs, and network engineers used to be rotated through the operations center to do just this. Furthermore, once fixes are made the organization should be quickly returned to a sense of preparedness for the next situation.

- **Deference to expertise**—During crisis events, shift the leadership role to the person possessing the greatest expertise to deal with the problem. Consider creating a competency around crisis management such as a "technical duty officer" in the operations center.

Never waste an opportunity to learn from your mistakes, as they are your greatest source of opportunity to make positive change. Put a process, such as a well run postmortem, in place to extract every ounce of learning that you can from your mistakes. If you have a well-designed system that fails infrequently, even under extreme scale, practice organizational "mindfulness" and get close to your data to better identify future failures easily. It is easy to be lured into a sense of complacency in these situations, and you are well served to hypothesize and brainstorm on different failure events that might happen.

Summary

This chapter has been about learning. Learn aggressively, learn from others' mistakes, learn from your own mistakes, and learn from your customers. Be a learning organization and a learning individual. The people and organizations that constantly learn will always be ahead of those who don't. As Charlie "Tremendous" Jones, the author of nine books and numerous awards, said, "In ten years you will be the same person you are today except for the people you meet and the books you read." We like to extend that thought that an organization will be the same tomorrow as they are today except for the lessons they learn from their customers, themselves, and others.

Endnotes

1. Charles Perrow, *Normal Accidents* (Princeton, NJ: Princeton University Press, 1999).

2. Todd R. LaPorte and Paula M. Consolini, "Working in Practice But Not in Theory: Theoretical Challenges of 'High-Reliability Organizations,'" *Journal of Public Administration Research and Theory*, Oxford Journals, http://jpart.oxfordjournals.org/content/1/1/19.extract.

3. Karl E. Weick and Kathleen M. Sutcliffe, "Managing the Unexpected," http://www.hetzwartegat.info/assets/files/Managing%20the%20Unexpected.pdf.

8

Database Rules

In Chapter 4, "Use the Right Tools," we discussed Maslow's Hammer (aka the Law of the Instrument), which put simply is an overreliance, to a fault, on a familiar tool. We discussed that one common example of overuse is the relational database. Recall that relational databases typically give us certain benefits outlined by an acronym called ACID described in Table 8.1.

Table 8.1 **ACID Properties of Databases**

Atomicity	All of the operations in the transaction will complete, or none will.
Consistency	The database will be in a consistent state when the transaction begins and ends.
Isolation	The transaction will behave as if it is the only operation being performed upon the database.
Durability	Upon completion of the transaction, the operation will not be reversed.

ACID properties are really powerful when we need to split up data into different entities with each entity having some number of relationships with other entities within the database. They are even more powerful when we want to process a large number of transactions through these entities and relationships; transactions consisting of reads of the data, updates to the data, the addition of new data (inserts or creates), and removal of certain data (deletes). While we should always strive to find more lightweight and faster ways to perform transactions, sometimes there simply

isn't an easy way around using a relational database, and sometimes the relational database is the best option for our implementation given the flexibility it affords. Whereas Rule 14
argued against using databases where they were not necessary,
this chapter when used in conjunction with the rules of Chapter
2 ("Distribute Your Work") helps us make the most out of databases without causing major scalability problems within our
architecture.

Rule 31—Be Aware of Costly Relationships

Rule 31: What, When, How, and Why

What: Be aware of relationships in the data model.

When to use: When designing the data model, adding
tables/columns, or writing queries consider how the relationships
between entities will affect performance and scalability in the
long run.

How to use: Think about database splits and possible future
data needs as you design the data model.

Why: The cost of fixing a broken data model after it has been
implemented is likely 100x as much as fixing it during the design
phase.

Key takeaways: Think ahead and plan the data model carefully.
Consider normalized forms, how you will likely split the database
in the future, and possible data needs of the application.

In our personal lives, unless we're masochistic, we all strive to
establish and build relationships that are balanced. Ideally we put
into a relationship roughly the same that we get out. When a
personal relationship becomes skewed in one person's favor the
other person may become unhappy, reevaluate the relationship,
and potentially end it. Although this book isn't about personal
relationships, the same cost = benefit balance that exists in our
personal relationships is applicable to our database relationships.

Database relationships are determined by the data model,
which captures the cardinality and referential integrity rules of
the data. To understand how this occurs and why it is important

we need to understand the basic steps involved in building a data model that results in the data definition language (DDL) statements that are used to actually create the physical structure to contain the data, that is, tables and columns. While there are all types of variations on this process, for a relational model the first step generally is to define the entities.

An entity is anything that can exist independently such as a physical object, event, or concept. Entities can have relationships with each other, and both the entity and the relationship can both have attributes describing them. Using the common grammar analogy, entities are nouns, relationships are verbs, and attributes are adjectives or adverbs, depending on what they modify.

Entities are single instances of something, such as a customer's purchase order, which can have attributes such as an order ID and total value. Grouping of the same type of entities together produces an entity set. In our database the entity is the equivalent of the row, and the entity set is the table. The unique attribute that describes the entity is the primary key of the table. Primary keys enforce entity integrity by uniquely identifying entity instances. The unique attributes that describe the relationship between entities are the foreign keys. Foreign keys enforce referential integrity by completing an association between two entities of different entity sets. Most commonly used to diagram entities, relationships and attributes are entity relationship diagrams (ERD). ERDs show the cardinality between entity sets, one-to-one, one-to-many, or many-to-many relationships.

Once the entities, relationships, and attributes are defined and mapped, the last step in the design of the data model is to consider normalization. The primary purpose of normalizing a data model is to ensure the data is stored in a manner that allows for insert, update, select, and delete (aka CRUD: Create Read Update Delete) with data integrity. Non-normalized data models have a high degree of data redundancy, which means that the risk of data integrity problems is greater. Normal forms build upon each other meaning that for a database to satisfy the requirements for second normal form it first must satisfy first normal form. The most common normal forms are described in the sidebar. If a database adheres to at least the third normal form it is considered normalized.

Normal Forms

Here are the most common normal forms used in databases. Each higher normal form implies that it must satisfy lower forms. Generally a database is said to be in normal form if it adheres to third normal form.

- **First normal form**—Originally, as defined by Codd,[1] the table should represent a relation and have no repeating groups. While "relation" is fairly well defined by Codd, the meaning of "repeating groups" is a source of debate. Controversy exists over whether tables are allowed to exist within tables and whether null fields are allowed. The most important concept is the ability to create a key.

- **Second normal form**—Nonkey fields cannot be described by only one of the keys in a composite key.

- **Third normal form**—All nonkey fields must be described by the key.

- **Boyce-Codd normal form**—Every determinant is a candidate key.

- **Fourth normal form**—A record type should not contain two or more multivalued facts.

- **Fifth normal form**—Every nontrivial join dependency in the table is implied by the candidate keys.

- **Sixth normal form**—No nontrivial join dependencies exist.

An easy mnemonic for the first three normal forms is "1 — The Key, 2 — The Whole Key, and 3 — Nothing But the Key."

As you have probably figured out by now, the relationships between entities dramatically affect how efficiently the data is stored, retrieved, and updated. It also plays a large role in scalability as these relationships define how we are able to split or shard our database. If we are attempting to perform a Y axis split of our database by pulling out the order confirmation service, this might prove problematic if the order entity is extensively related to other entities. Trying to untangle this web of relationships is difficult after the fact. It is well worth the time spent up front in the design phase to save you 10x or 100x the effort when you need to split your databases.

One last aspect of data relationships that is important to scalability is how we join tables in our queries. This, of course, is also very much dictated by the data model but also by our developers who are creating reports, new pages in our applications, and so on. We won't attempt to cover the steps to query optimization in detail here, but suffice it to say that new queries should be reviewed by a competent DBA who is familiar with the data model, and should be analyzed for performance characteristics prior to being placed into the production environment.

You have probably noticed that there is a relationship between a desire for increased data integrity through normalization and the degree to which relationships must be used in a database. The higher the normal form, the greater the number of potential relationships as we create tables specific to such things as repeating values. What was once taught as a law years ago in database design (moving up in normal form is good) is now seen as more of a tradeoff in high transaction system design. This tradeoff is similar to the tradeoff between risk and cost, cost and quality, time and cost, and so on; specifically a decrease in one side typically implies an increase in the other. Often to increase scale, we look to reduce normal forms.

When SQL queries perform poorly because of the requirements to join tables there are several alternatives. The first is to tune the query. If this doesn't help another alternative is to create a view, materialized view, summary table, and so on that can preprocess the joins. Another alternative is to not join in the query but rather pull the data sets into the application and join in memory in the application. While this is more complex it removes the processing of the join off the database, which is often the most difficult to scale and puts it in the application server tier, which is easier to scale out with more commodity hardware. A final alternative is to push back on the business requirements. Often our business partners will come up with different solutions when it is explained that the way they have requested the report requires a 10% increase in hardware while the removal of a single column may make the report trivial in complexity and nearly as equivalent in business value.

Rule 32—Use the Right Type of Database Lock

> ### Rule 32: What, When, How, and Why
>
> **What**: Be cognizant of the use of explicit locks and monitor implicit locks.
>
> **When to use**: Anytime you employ relational databases for your solution.
>
> **How to use**: Monitor explicit locks in code reviews. Monitor databases for implicit locks and adjust explicitly as necessary to moderate throughput. Choose a database and storage engine that allows flexibility in types and granularity of locking.
>
> **Why**: Maximize concurrency and throughput in databases within your environment.
>
> **Key takeaways**: Understand the types of locks and manage their usage to maximize database throughput and concurrency. Change lock types to get better utilization of databases and look to split schemas or distribute databases as you grow. When choosing databases, ensure you choose one that allows multiple lock types and granularity to maximize concurrency.

Locks are a fact of life within a database; they are the way in which databases allow concurrent users while helping to ensure the consistency and isolation components of the ACID properties of a database. But there are many different types of database locks, and even different approaches to implementing them. Table 8.2 offers a brief and high-level overview of different lock types supported in many different open source and third-party proprietary database management systems. Not all of these locks are supported by all databases, and the lock types can be mixed. For instance, a row lock can be either explicit or implicit.

Table 8.2   **Lock Types**

Type of Lock	Description
Implicit	Implicit locks are those generated by the database on behalf of a user to perform certain transactions. These are typically generated when necessary for certain DML (Data Manipulation Language) tasks.

Type of Lock	Description
Explicit	These are locks defined by the user of a database during the course of his interaction with entities within the database.
Row	Row level locking locks a row in a table of a database that is being updated, read, or created.
Page	Page level locking locks the entire page that contains a row or group of rows being updated.
Extent	Typically, these are locks on groups of pages. They are common when database space is being added.
Table	Locks an entire table (an entity within a database).
Database	Locks the entirety of entities and relationships within a database.

If you search a bit, you will find many other types of locks. There are, depending on the type of database, key and index locks that work on the indices that you create over your tables. You may also find a discussion of column locking and ways in which different databases might support that notion. To our knowledge, few if any databases actually support this type of locking, and if it is supported it isn't used very frequently within the industry.

While locking is absolutely critical to the operations of a database to facilitate both isolation and consistency, it is obviously costly. Typically databases allow reads to occur simultaneously on data, while blocking all reads during the course of a write (an update or insertion) on an element undergoing an operation. Reads then can occur very fast, and many of them can happen at one time while typically a write happens in isolation. The finer the granularity of the write operation, such as in the case of a single row, the more of these can happen within the database or even within a table at a time. Increasing the granularity of the object being written or updated, such as updating multiple rows at a time, may require an escalation of the type of lock necessary.

The size or granularity of lock to employ ultimately impacts the throughput of transactions. When updating many rows at a single time within a database, the cost of acquiring multiple row locks and the competition for these rows might result in fewer transactions per second than just acquiring a larger lock of a page, extent, or table. But if too large a lock is grabbed, such as a page when only updating a small number of rows, then transaction throughput will decrease while the lock is held.

Often a component of the database (commonly called an *optimizer* within many databases) determines what size of element should be locked in an attempt to allow maximum concurrency while ensuring consistency and isolation. In most cases, initially allowing the optimizer to determine what should be locked is your best course of action. This component of the database has more knowledge about what is likely to be updated than you do at the time of the operation. Unfortunately, these systems are bound to make mistakes, and this is where it is critical that we monitor our databases in production and make changes to our DML to make it more efficient as we learn from what happens in our production environments.

Most databases allow performance statistics to be collected that allow us to understand the most common locking conditions and the most common events causing transactions to wait before being processed. By analyzing this information historically, and by monitoring these events aggressively in the production environment, we can identify when the optimizer is incorrectly identifying the type of lock it should use and force the database to use an appropriate type of locking. For instance, if through our analysis we identify that our database is consistently using table locking for a particular table and we believe we would get greater concurrency out of row level locking, we might be able to force this change.

Perhaps as important as the analysis of what is causing bottlenecks and what type of locking we should employ is the notion of determining if we can change the entity relationships to reduce contention and increase concurrency. This of course brings us back to the concepts we discussed in Chapter 2. We can, for instance, split our reads across multiple copies of the database and force writes to a single copy as in the X axis of scale (Rule 7). Or we can split up our tables across multiple databases based partially on contention such as in the Y axis of scale (Rule 8). Finally, we may just reduce table size by pulling out certain customer-specific data into multiple tables to allow the contention to be split across these entities such as in the Z axis of scale (Rule 9).

Finally, where we employ databases to do our work we should try to ensure we are choosing the best solution. As we've said time and again, we believe that you can scale nearly any product using nearly any set of technologies. That said, most decisions we make will have an impact on either our cost of operating our product or our time to market. There are, for example, some database storage engine solutions that limit the types of locks we can employ within the database, and as a result limit our ability to tune our databases to maximize concurrent transactions. MySQL is an example where the selection of a storage engine such as MyISAM can limit you to table level locks and, as a result, potentially limits your transaction throughput.

Rule 33—Pass on Using Multiphase Commits

Rule 33: What, When, How, and Why

What: Do not use a multiphase commit protocol to store or process transactions.

When to use: Always pass or alternatively "never use" multiphase commits.

How to use: Don't use it; split your data storage and processing systems with Y or Z axis splits.

Why: Multiphase commits are blocking protocols that do not permit other transactions from occurring until it is complete.

Key takeaways: Do not use multiphase commit protocols as a simple way to extend the life of your monolithic database. It will likely cause it to scale even less and result in an even earlier demise of your system.

Multiphase commit protocols, which include the popular
two-phase commit (2PC) and three-phase commit (3PC), are
specialized consensus protocols. The purpose of these protocols is
to coordinate processes that participate in a distributed atomic
transaction to determine whether to commit or abort (roll back)
the transaction.[2] Because of these algorithms' capability to
handle systemwide failures of the network or processes, they
are often looked to as solutions for distributed data storage or
processing.

The basic algorithm of 2PC consists of two phases. The first
phase, voting phase, is where the master storage or coordinator
makes a "commit request" to all the cohorts or other storage
devices. All the cohorts process the transaction up to the point of
committing and then acknowledge that they can commit or vote
"yes." Thus begins the second phase or completion phase, where
the master sends a commit signal to all cohorts who begin the
commit of the data. If any cohorts should fail during the commit then a rollback is sent to all cohorts and the transaction is
abandoned. An example of this protocol is shown in Figure 8.1.

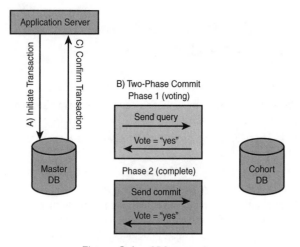

Figure 8.1   2PC example

So far this protocol probably sounds pretty good since it provides atomicity of transactions within a distributed database environment. Hold off on your judgment just a short while longer. In the example Figure 8.1, notice that the app server initiated the transaction, step A. Then all the 2PC steps started happening and had to complete, step B, before the master database could acknowledge back to the app server that indeed that transaction was completed, step C. During that entire time the app server thread was held up waiting for the SQL query to complete and the database to acknowledge the transaction. This example is typical of almost any consumer purchase, registration, or bidding transaction on the Web where you might try to implement 2PC. Unfortunately, locking up the app server for that long can have dire consequences. While you might think that you either have plenty of capacity on your app servers or that you can scale them out pretty cost effectively since they are commodity hardware, the locking also occurs on the database. Because you're committing, all rows of data, assuming you have row-level locking capabilities because it's even worse for block level, you are locking up all those rows until everything commits and gives the "all clear."

We've implemented (or rather failed to implement) 2PC on a large scale, and the results were disastrous and entirely due to the lock and wait nature of the approach. Our database could initially handle thousands of reads and writes a second prior to the 2PC implementation. After introducing 2PC for just a fraction of the calls (less than 2%), the site completely locked up before processing a quarter of the total number of transactions it could previously handle. While we could have added more application servers, the database was not able to process more queries because of locks on the data.

While 2PC might seem like a good alternative to actually splitting your database by a Y or Z axis split (Rules 8 and 9), think again. Pull (or separate) database tables apart the smart way instead of trying to extend the life of your monolithic database with a multiphase commit protocol.

Rule 34—Try Not to Use "Select For Update"

Rule 34: What, When, How, and Why

What: Minimize the use of the FOR UPDATE clause in a SELECT statement when declaring cursors.

When to use: Always.

How to use: Review cursor development and question every SELECT FOR UPDATE usage.

Why: Use of FOR UPDATE causes locks on rows and may slow down transactions.

Key takeaways: Cursors are powerful constructs that when properly used can actually make programming faster and easier while speeding up transactions. But FOR UPDATE cursors may cause long held locks and slow transactions. Refer to your database documentation for whether you need to use the FOR READ ONLY clause to minimize locks.

When leveraged properly, cursors are powerful database control structures that allow us to traverse and process data within some result set defined by the query (or operation) of the cursor. Cursors are useful when we plan to specify some set of data and "cursor through" or process the rows in the data set in an iterative fashion. Items within the data set can be updated, deleted, or modified or simply read and reviewed for other processing. The real power of the cursor is as an extension of the capability of the programming language, as many procedural and object-oriented programming languages don't offer built-in capabilities of managing data sets within a relational database. One potentially troublesome approach in very high transaction systems is the FOR UPDATE clause in SELECT cursors as we often are not in control of how long the cursor will be active, the resulting lock on records can cause slow-downs or even near deadlock scenarios in our product.

In many databases, when the cursor with a FOR UPDATE clause is opened, the rows identified within the statement are locked until either a commit or rollback is issued within the session. The COMMIT statement saves changes and a ROLLBACK cancels any changes. With the issuing of either statement, the locks associated with the rows in the database are released. Additionally, after issuing the commit or rollback, you lose your position within the cursor and will not be able to execute any more fetches against it.

Pause for a second now and think back to Rule 32 and our discussion of database locks. Can you identify at least two potential problems with the "Select for Update" cursor? The first problem is that the cursor holds locks on rows within the database while you perform your actions. Granted, in many cases this might be useful, and in some smaller number of cases it might either be unavoidable or may be the best approach for the solution. But these locks are going to potentially cause other transactions to block or wait while you perform some number of actions. If these actions are complex or take some time you may stack up a great number of pending transactions. If these other transactions also happen to be cursors expecting to perform a "select for update" we may create a wait queue that simply will not be processed within our users' acceptable timeframe. In a Web environment, impatient users waiting on slowly responding requests may issue additional requests with the notion that per- haps the subsequent requests will complete more quickly. The result is a disaster; our systems come to a halt as pending requests stack up on the database and ultimately cause our Web servers to fill up their TCP ports and stop responding to users.

The second problem is the mirror image of our first problem and hinted at previously. Future cursors desiring a lock on one or more rows that are currently locked will wait until other locks clear. Note that these locks don't necessarily need to be placed by other cursors; they can be explicit locks from users or implicit locks from the RDBMS. The more locking that we have going on within the database, even while some of it is likely necessary, the more likely we will have transactions backing up. Very long held locks will engender slower response times for frequently requested data. Some databases, such as Oracle, include the optional keyword "NOWAIT" that releases control back to the process to perform other work or to wait before try- ing to reacquire the lock. But if the cursor must be processed for some synchronous user request, the end result to the user is the same—a long wait for a client request.

Be aware that some databases default to "for update" for cursors. In fact, the American National Standards Institute (ANSI) SQL standard indicates that any cursor should default to FOR UPDATE unless it includes the clause FOR READ ONLY on the DECLARE statement. Developers and DBAs should refer to their database documentation to identify how to develop cursors with minimal locks.

Rule 35—Don't Select Everything

Rule 35: What, When, How, and Why

What: Don't use Select * in queries.

When to use: Always use this rule (or put another way, never select everything).

How to use: Always declare what columns of data you are selecting or inserting in a query.

Why: Selecting everything in a query is prone to break things when the table structure changes and it transfers unneeded data.

Key takeaways: Don't use wildcards when selecting or inserting data.

This is a pretty simple and straightforward rule. For most of us the first SQL we learned was

```
Select * from table_name_blah;
```

When it returned a bunch of data we were thrilled. Unfortunately, some of our developers either never moved beyond this point or regressed back to it over the years. Selecting everything is fast and simple but really never a good idea. There are several problems with this that we'll cover, but keep in mind that this mentality of selecting unnamed data can be seen in another DML statement, Insert.

There are two primary problems with the Select *. The first is the probability of data mapping problems, and the second is the transfer of unnecessary data. When we execute a select query we're often expecting to display or manipulate that data and to do so requires that we map the data into some type of

variable. In the following code example there are two functions,
bad_qry_data and good_qry_data. As the name should give
away, bad_qry_data is a bad example of how you can map a
query into an array, and good_qry_data shows a better way of
doing it. In both functions, we are selecting the values from the
table bestpostpage and mapping them into a two-dimensional
array. Since we know there are four columns in the table we
might feel that we're safe using the bad_qry_data function. The
problem is when the next developer needs to add a column to
the table they might issue a command such as this:

```
ALTER TABLE bestpostpage ADD remote_host varchar(25) AFTER id;
```

The result is that your mapping from column 1 is no longer the
remote_ip but instead is now remote_host. A better solution
is to simply declare all the variables that you are selecting and
identify them by name when mapping.

```
function bad_qry_data() {
  $sql = "SELECT * "
    . "FROM bestpostpage "
    . "ORDER BY insert_date DESC LIMIT 100";
  $qry_results = exec_qry($sql);
  $i = 0;
  while($row = mysql_fetch_array($qry_results)) {
      $ResArr[$i]["id"] = $row[0];
      $ResArr[$i]["remote_ip"] = $row[1];
      $ResArr[$i]["post_data"] = $row[2];
      $ResArr[$i]["insert_date"] = $row[3];
      $i++;
  } // while
  return $ResArr;
} //function qry_data

function good_qry_data() {
  $sql = "SELECT id, remote_ip, post_data, insert_date "
    . "FROM bestpostpage "
    . "ORDER BY insert_date DESC LIMIT 100";
  $qry_results = exec_qry($sql);
  $i = 0;
  while($row = mysql_fetch_assoc($qry_results)) {
   $ResArr[$i]["id"] = $row["id"];
```

```
    $ResArr[$i]["remote_ip"] = $row["remote_ip"];
    $ResArr[$i]["post_data"] = $row["post_data"];
    $ResArr[$i]["insert_date"] = $row["insert_date"];
    $i++;
  } // while
  return $ResArr;
} //function qry_data
```

The second big problem with `Select` `*` is that usually you
don't need all the data in all the columns. While the actual
lookup of additional columns isn't resource consuming, the
transfer of all that additional data from the database server to the
application server can add up to significant amounts when that
query gets executed dozens or even hundreds of times per
minute for different users.

Lest you think this is all about the much-maligned `Select`
statement, `Insert` can fall prey to the exact same problem of
unspecified columns. The following SQL statement is perfectly
valid as long as the column count of the table matches the number of values being entered. This will break when an additional
column is added to the table, which might cause an issue with
your system but should be able to be caught early in testing.

```
INSERT INTO bestpostpage VALUES (1, '10.97.23.45', 'test
data', '2010-11-19 11:15:00');
```

A much better way of inserting the data is to use the actual column names, like this:

```
INSERT INTO bestpostpage (id, remote_ip, post_data,
insert_date) VALUES (1, '10.97.23.45', 'test data',
'2010-11-19 11:15:00');
```

As a best practice, do not get in the habit of using `Select` or
`Insert` without specifying the columns. Besides wasting
resources and being likely to break or potentially even corrupt
data, it also prevents you from rolling back. As we discussed in
Rule 29 building the capability to roll back is critical to both
scalability and availability.

Summary

In this chapter we discussed rules that will help your database scale. Ideally, we'd like to avoid the use of relational databases because they are more difficult to scale than other parts of systems, but sometimes their use is unavoidable. Given that the database is often the most difficult part of the application to scale, particular attention should be paid to these rules. When the rules presented in this chapter are combined with rules from other chapters such as Chapter 2, you should have a strong base of do's and don'ts to ensure your database scales.

Endnotes

1. E. F. Codd, "A Relationship Model of Data for Large Shared Data Banks," *Communications of the ACM* 13 (6): 377-387.
2. Wikipedia, "Two-phase commit," http://en.wikipedia.org/wiki/Two-phase_commit_protocol.

9

Design for Fault Tolerance and Graceful Failure

In our experience, the second most common scalability related failure behind "Not designed to scale" is "Not designed to fail." While this may sound a bit odd, it is in fact the most common type of scale failure in sites that are designed to be nearly infinitely scalable. Very often, small unexpected failures of certain key features will back up transactions and bring the whole business to its knees. After all, what good is a site that can scale infinitely if it isn't resilient to failures? We all know that there is no way around systems or software failing, and as we add systems and software, our rate of failure will increase. While increasing our number of systems and associated services 1000x may not result in 1000x more failures, we should expect some significant increase. If we can't handle this increase in failures, have we really delivered on the promise of scalability to our business? We think not.

In our business, availability and scalability go hand in hand. A product that isn't highly available really doesn't need to scale and a site that can't scale won't be highly available when the demand comes. As such, you really can't work on one without thinking about the other. This chapter offers rules that help ensure sites can both scale AND be resilient to and tolerant of failures while still delivering value to the customer.

Rule 36—Design Using Fault Isolative "Swimlanes"

Rule 36: What, When, How, and Why

What: Implement fault isolation or *swimlanes* in your designs.

When to use: Whenever you are beginning to split up databases to scale.

How to use: Split up databases and services along the Y or Z axis and disallow synchronous communication or access between services.

Why: Increase availability and scalability and reduce incident identification and resolution as well as time to market and cost.

Key takeaways: Fault isolation consists of eliminating synchronous calls between fault isolation domains, limiting asynchronous calls and handling synchronous call failure, and eliminating the sharing of services and data between swimlanes.

Our terminology in splitting up services and data is rich with confusing and sometimes conflicting terms. Different organizations often use words such as *pod*, *pool*, *cluster*, and *shard*. Adding to this confusion is that these terms are often used interchangeably by the same organization. In one context, a team may use "shard" to identify groupings of services and data while in another it only means the separation of data within a database. Given the confusion and differentiation in usage of the existing terms, we created the term *swimlane* in our practice to try to hammer home the important concept of fault isolation. While some of our clients started adopting the term to indicate fault isolative splits of services or customer segmentation in production, its most important contribution is in the design arena. Table 9.1 is a list of common terms, their most common descriptions, and an identification of how and when they are used interchangeably in practice.

Table 9.1 **Types of Splits**

Split Name	Description
Pod	Pods are self-contained sets of functionality containing app servers, persistent storage (such as a database or other persistent and shared file system), or both. Pods are most often splits along the Z axis, as in a split of customers into separate pods. "Pod" is sometimes used interchangeably with the term "swimlane." It has also been used interchangeably with the term "pool" when referring to Web or application services.
Cluster	Clusters are sometimes used for Web and application servers in the same fashion as a "pool" identified next. In these cases a cluster refers to an X axis scale of similar functionality or purpose configured such that all nodes or participants are "active." Often a cluster will share some sort of distributed state above and beyond that of a pool, but this state can cause scalability bottlenecks under high transaction volumes. Clusters might also refer to active/passive configuration where one (or more) devices sit "passive" and become "active" on the failure of a peer device.
Pool	Pools are servers that group similar functionality or potentially separate groups of customers. The term typically refers to front end servers, but some companies refer to database service pools for certain characteristics. Pools are typically X axis replicated (cloned) servers that are demarcated by function (Y axis) or customer (Z axis).
Shard	Shards are horizontal partitions of databases or search engines. Horizontal partitioning means the separation of data across database tables, database instances, or physical database servers. Shards typically occur along the Z axis of scale (for instance splitting up customers among shards), but some companies refer to functional (Y axis) splits as shards as well.
Swimlane	A swimlane is a term used to identify a fault isolation domain. Synchronous calls are never allowed across swimlane boundaries. Put another way, a swimlane is defined around a set of synchronous calls. The failure of a component within one swimlane does not affect components in other swimlanes. As such, no component is shared across swimlanes.

From our perspective, the most important differentiation among these terms is the notion of design. Whereas pool, shard, cluster, and pod might refer to either how something is implemented in a production environment or how one might split up customers or services, swimlane is a design concept around creating fault isolation domains. A fault isolation domain is an area in which, should a physical or logical service fail to work appropriately, whether that failure is in a slow response time or an absolute failure to respond, the only services affected are those within the failure domain. Swimlanes extend the concepts provided within shards and pods by extending the failure domain to the front door of your services—the entry into your data center. At the extreme it means providing separate Web, application, and database servers by function or fault isolation zone. At its heart, a swimlane is about both scalability and availability, rather than just a mechanism by which one can scale transactions.

We borrowed the concept from CSMA/CD (carrier sense multiple access with collision detection—commonly referred to as Ethernet), where fault isolation domains were known as collision domains. To offset the effects of collisions in the days before full duplex switches, Ethernet segments would contain collisions such that their effects weren't felt by all attached systems. We felt the term *swimlane* was a great metaphor for fault isolation as in pools the lines between lanes of swimmers help keep those swimmers from interfering with each other during the course of their swim. Similarly, "lines" between groupings of customers or functionality across which synchronous transactions do not occur, can help ensure that failures in one lane don't adversely affect the operations of other lanes.

The benefits of fault isolative swimlanes go beyond the notion of increasing availability through the isolation of faults. Because swimlanes segment customers and/or functionality shared across customers, when failures occur you can more quickly identify the source. If you've performed a Z axis segmentation of your customers from your Web servers through your persistence tier, a failure that is unique to a single customer will quickly be isolated to the set of customers in that swimlane. You'll know you are looking for a bug or issue that is triggered by data or actions unique to the customers in that swimlane. If you've performed a Y axis segmentation and the "shopping cart" swimlane has a problem, you'll know immediately that the problem is associated with either the code, database, or servers comprising that swimlane. Incident detection and resolution as well as problem detection and resolution both clearly benefit from fault isolation.

Other benefits from fault isolation include better scalability, faster time to market, and lower cost. Because we focus on partitioning our systems, we begin to think of scaling horizontally, and hence our scalability increases. If we've separated our swimlanes by the Y axis of scale, we can separate our code base and make more efficient use of our engineers as discussed in Chapter 2, "Distribute Your Work." As such, we get better engineering throughput and therefore lower cost per unit developed. And if we are getting greater throughput, we are obviously delivering our product to market faster. Ultimately all of these benefits allow us to handle the "expected but unexpected": those things that we know will happen sooner or later but which we cannot clearly identify the impact. In other words, we know things are going to break we just don't know what will break or when it will happen. Fault isolation allows us to more gracefully handle these failures. Table 9.2 summarizes the benefits of fault isolation (or swimlanes).

Table 9.2   **Fault Isolation Benefits**

Area	Benefit
Availability	Availability is increased as a failure within one failure domain does not impact other services (Y axis) or other customers (Z axis) depending on how the swimlane is architected.
Incident detection	Incidents are detected faster as fewer components or services need to be investigated during an event. Isolation helps identify what exactly is failing.
Scalability	Horizontal scale is achieved when fault isolated services can grow independently of each other.
Cost	Development cost is reduced through higher engineer throughput achieved from focus and specialization.
Time to market	As throughput increases, time to market for functions decreases.

Having discussed why we should swimlane or fault isolate our product offerings, we turn our attention to the more important question of how to achieve fault isolation. We rely on four principles that both define swimlanes and help us in designing them. The first is that nothing is shared between swimlanes. We typically exempt major network components such as inbound border routers and some core routers but include switches unique to the service being fault isolated. It is also common to share some other devices such as a very large switched storage area network or load balancers in a smaller site. Wherever possible, and within your particular cost constraints, try to share as little as possible. Databases and servers should never be shared. Because swimlanes are partially defined by a lack of sharing, the sharing of servers and databases is always the starting point for identifying where swimlane boundaries truly exist. Due to the costs of network gear and storage subsystems these are sometimes shared across swimlanes during the initial phases of growth.

The second principle of swimlanes is that no synchronous calls happen between swimlanes. Because synchronous calls tie services together, the failure of a service being called can propagate to all other systems calling it in a synchronous and blocking fashion. Therefore, it would violate the notion of fault isolation if a failure of a service we hoped to be in one swimlane could cause the failure of a service in another swimlane.

The third principle limits asynchronous calls between swimlanes. While asynchronous calls are much less likely than synchronous calls to propagate failures across systems, there still exists an opportunity to reduce our availability with these calls. Sudden surges in requests may make certain systems slow, such as in the case of messages being generated subsequent to a denial of service attack. An overwhelming number of these messages may back up queues, start to fill up TCP ports, and even bring database processing of synchronous requests to a standstill if not properly implemented. As such, we try to limit the number of these transactions crossing swimlane boundaries.

The last principle of swimlanes addresses how to implement asynchronous transmissions across swimlane boundaries when they are absolutely necessary. Put simply, anytime we are going to communicate asynchronously across a swimlane, we need the ability to "just not care" about the transaction. In some cases, we may timeout the transaction and forget about it. Potentially we are just "informing" another swimlane of some action, and we don't care to get a response at all. In all cases we should implement logic to "wire off" or "toggle off" the communication based on a manual switch, an automatic switch, or both. Our communications should be able to be switched off by someone monitoring the system and identifying a failure (the manual switch) and should sense when things aren't going well and stop communicating (the automatic switche

These principles are summarized in Table 9.3.

Table 9.3   **Fault Isolation Principles**

Principle	Description
Share nothing	Swimlanes should not share services. Some sharing of network gear such as border routers and load balancers is acceptable. If necessary, storage area networks can be shared. Databases and servers should never be shared.
No synchronous calls between swimlanes	Synchronous calls are never allowed across swimlane boundaries. Put another way, a swimlane is the smallest unit across which no synchronous calls happen.
Limit asynchronous calls between swimlanes	Asynchronous calls should be limited across swimlanes. They are permitted, but the more calls that are made, the greater the chance of failure propagation.
Use timeouts and Wire-On/Wire-Off with asynchronous calls	Asynchronous calls should be implemented with timeouts and the ability to turn off the call when necessary due to failures in other services. See Rule 39.

How about the case where we want fault isolation but need synchronous communication or access to another data source? In the former case, we can duplicate the service that we believe we need and put it in our swimlane. Payment gateways are one example of this type of approach. If we were to swimlane along a Z axis by customer, we probably don't want each of our customer swimlanes synchronously (blocking) calling a single payment gateway for a service like checkout. We could simply implement N payment gateways where N is the degree of customer segmentations or number of customer swimlanes.

What if there is some shared information to which we need access in each of these swimlanes such as in the case of login credentials? Maybe we have separated authentication and signin/login into its own Y axis split, but we need to reference the associated credentials from time to time on a read-only basis within each customer (Z axis) swimlane. We often use read replicas of databases for such purposes, putting one read replica in each swimlane. Many databases offer this replication technology out of the box, and even allow you to slice it up into smaller pieces, meaning that we don't need to duplicate 100% of the customer data in each of our swimlanes. Some customers cache relevant information for read-only purposes in distributed object caches within the appropriate swimlane.

One question that we commonly get is how to implement swimlanes in a virtualized server world. Virtualization adds a new dimension to fault isolation—the dimension of logical (or virtual) in addition to physical failures. If virtualization is implemented primarily to split up larger machines into smaller ones, then you should continue to view the physical server as the swimlane boundary. In other words, don't mix virtual servers from different swimlanes on the same physical device. Some of our customers, however, have such a variety of product offerings with varying demand characteristics of the year that they rely on virtualization as a way of flexing capacity across these product offerings. In these cases, we try to limit the number of swimlanes mixed on a virtual server. Ideally, you would flex an entire physical server in and out of a swimlane rather than mix swimlanes on that server.

Swimlanes and Virtualization

When using virtualization to carve larger servers into smaller servers, attempt to keep swimlanes along physical server boundaries. Mixing virtual servers from different swimlanes on one physical server eliminates many of the fault isolative benefits of a swimlane.

Rule 37—Never Trust Single Points of Failure

Rule 37: What, When, How, and Why

What: Never implement and always eliminate single points of failure.

When to use: During architecture reviews and new designs.

How to use: Identify single instances on architectural diagrams. Strive for active/active configurations.

Why: Maximize availability through multiple instances.

Key takeaways: Strive for active/active rather than active/passive solutions. Use load balancers to balance traffic across instances of a service. Use control services with active/passive instances for patterns that require singletons.

In mathematics, singletons are sets that have only one element {A}. In programming parlance, the singleton pattern is a design pattern that mimics the mathematical notion and restricts the instantiation of a class to only one object. This design pattern is useful for coordination of a resource but is often overused by developers in an effort to be expeditious—more on this later. In system architecture, the singleton pattern, or more aptly the singleton *antipattern*, is known as a single point of failure (SPOF). This is when there exists only one instance of a component within a system that when it fails will cause a systemwide incident.

SPOFs can be anywhere in the system from a single Web server or single network device but most often the SPOF in a system is the database. The reason for this is that the database is often the most difficult to scale across multiple nodes and therefore gets left as a singleton. In Figure 9.1, even though there are redundant login, search, and checkout servers the database is a SPOF. What makes it worse is that all the service pools are reliant on that single database. While any SPOF is bad, the bigger problem with a database as a SPOF is if the database slows down or crashes, all services pools with synchronous calls to that database will also experience an incident.

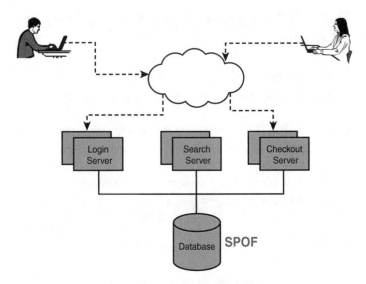

Figure 9.1   Database SPOF

We have a mantra that we share with our clients, and it is simply "everything fails." This goes for servers, storage systems, network devices, and datacenters. If you can name it, it can fail, and we've probably seen it happen. While most people think of datacenters as never failing, we have personal experience with more than a dozen datacenter outages in as many years. The same goes for highly available storage area networks. While they are remarkably more reliable than the old SCSI disk arrays, they still can and do fail.

The solution to most SPOFs is simply requisitioning another piece of hardware and running two or more of every service by cloning that service as described in our X axis of scale. Unfortunately, this isn't always so easy. Let's retrace our steps to the programming singleton pattern. While not all singleton class-es will prevent you from running a service on multiple servers, some implementations absolutely will prevent you from this without dire consequences. As a simplified example, if we have a class in our code that handles the subtraction of funds from a user's account this might be implemented as a singleton to prevent unpleasant things from happening to a user's balance such as it going negative. If we place this code on two separate servers without additional controls or semaphores it is possible that two simultaneous transactions attempt to debit a users account, which could lead to erroneous or undesired conditions. In this case we need to either fix the code to handle this condition or rely on an external control to prevent this condition. While the most desirable solution is to fix the code so that the service can be implemented on many different hosts, often we need an expeditious fix to remove a SPOF. As the last focus of this rule, we'll discuss a few of these quick fixes next.

The first and simplest solution is to use an active-passive configuration. The service would run actively on one server and passively (not taking traffic) on a second server. This hot/cold configuration is often used with databases as a first step in removing a SPOF. The next alternative would be to use another component in the system to control the access to data. If the SPOF was a service, then the database can be used to control access to data through the use of locks. If the SPOF is the database, a master-slave configuration can be set up, and the application can control access to the data with writes/updates going to the master and reads/selects going to the slave. A last configuration that can be used to fix a SPOF is a load balancer. If the service on a Web or application server was a SPOF and could not be eliminated in code the load balancer can often be used to fix a user's request to only one server in the pool. This is done through session cookies, which are set on the user's browser and allow the load balancer to redirect that user's requests to the same Web or application server each time resulting in a consistent state.

We covered several alternative solutions to SPOFs that can be implemented quickly when code changes cannot be made in a timely manner. While the best and final solution should be to fix the code to allow for multiple instances of the service to run on different physical servers the first step is to eliminate the SPOF as soon as possible. Remember, "everything fails" so don't be surprised when your SPOF fails.

Rule 38—Avoid Putting Systems in Series

> ### Rule 38: What, When, How, and Why
>
> **What:** Reduce the number of components that are connected in series.
>
> **When to use:** Anytime you are considering adding components.
>
> **How to use:** Remove unnecessary components or add multiple versions of them to minimize the impact.
>
> **Why:** Components in series have a multiplicative effect of failure.
>
> **Key takeaways:** Avoid adding components to your system that are connected in series. When necessary to do so add multiple versions of that component so that if one fails others are available to take its place.

Components in electrical circuits can be connected in a variety of ways; the two simplest are series and parallel. Circuits in series have components such as resistors and capacitors that are connected along a single path. In this type of circuit the current flows through every component, and the resistance and voltage are additive. Figure 9.2 shows two circuits one with three resistors and one with three batteries and the resulting resistance and voltage. Notice that in this diagram if any of the components fail, such as a resistor blows, then the entire circuit fails.

Figure 9.3 shows two parallel circuits, the top one with three resistors (and a voltage source or capacitor) and the bottom one with three batteries. In this circuit, the total resistance is calculated by summing the reciprocals of each resistance and then taking the reciprocal of that sum. The total resistance by definition must be less than the smallest resistance. Notice also that the voltage does not change but instead the batteries only contribute a fraction of the current, which has the effect of extending their useful life. Notice that in these circuits the failure of a component does not cause a failure across the entire circuit.

The similarities between the architecture of your system and a circuit are many. Your servers and network gear are components. Some components in your system are Web servers, some are application servers, some are load balancers, and others are database servers. These can be connected in parallel or in series. As a simple example let's take a static Web site that has a lot of traffic. You could put ten Web servers all with the same static site on them to serve traffic. You could either use a load balancer to direct traffic or assign all ten separate IP addresses that you associate with your domain through DNS. These Web servers are connected in parallel just like the batteries in Figure 9.3. The total current or amount of traffic that one Web server has to handle is a fraction of the total, and if one Web server fails the site remains available as it still has nine other Web servers.

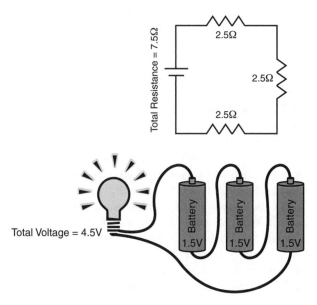

Figure 9.2   Circuits in series

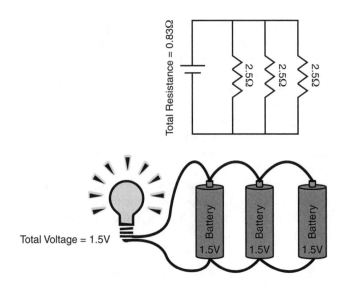

Figure 9.3   Circuits in parallel

As an example of a more typical architecture in series, let's add some layers. If we take a standard three tier site that has a single Web server, one application server, and one database server then we have an architecture connected in series. For a request to be fulfilled, the Web server must accept it and pass a request to the application server, which queries the database. The application server then receives the data back, manipulates the data, and sends it back to the Web server, which finally fulfills the request to the customer. If any component in this circuit or architecture breaks, then the entire system is down.

This brings us back to your real world architecture. Almost always there are going to be requirements to have components in series. When you take into consideration the load balancer, the Web and application tier, the database, the storage system, and so on there are many components required to keep your system running. Certainly adding components in parallel, even when tiers are connected in series, helps reduce the risk of total system failure caused by a component failure. Multiple Web servers spread the traffic load and prevent a system failure if only one Web server fails. On the Web and application tiers most people readily acknowledge this concept. Where most people overlook this problem is in the database and network layers. If Web and application servers connected in parallel all are connected in series to a single database we can have a single component result in catastrophic failure. This is why it is important to pay attention to the rules in Chapter 2 about splitting your database and in Chapter 3, "Design to Scale Out Horizontally," about scaling horizontally.

In regards to the network components we often see architectures that pay a lot of attention to connecting servers in parallel but completely ignore the network devices, especially firewalls. It is not uncommon to see firewalls inside and outside the network; see Rule 15 for further discussion regarding firewalls. In this case we have traffic going through a firewall, through a load balancer, through a firewall, through a switch, then to a Web server, an application server, a database server, and all the way back. There are at least seven components twice. So what's the big deal about adding another component if you're already going through a half dozen?

Items in series have a *multiplicity effect* on risk of failure. As a simple example if we have two servers in series, each with a 99.9% availability or uptime, then our total availability of the system cannot be greater than 99.9% × 99.9% = 99.8%. If we add a third component, in series, at the same 3-9's availability of 99.9% we get an even lower availability of 99.9% × 99.9% × 99.9% = 99.7%. The more components that are placed in series, the lower the system's availability. Table 9.4 lists some simple calculations that demonstrate the lowered availability and the resulting increase in downtime per month. For every component (at 99.9% availability) that we add to the system in series, we are adding ~43 minutes of downtime per month.

Table 9.4   **Components in Series at 99.9% Availability**

# of Components in Series	Total Availability	Minutes of Downtime per Month
1	99.9%	43.2
2	99.8%	86.4
3	99.7%	129.5
4	99.6%	172.5
5	99.5%	215.6
6	99.4%	258.6
7	99.3%	301.5
8	99.2%	344.4
9	99.1%	387.2

Because your system, just like most circuits today, are much more complicated than a simple series or parallel connection, the exact calculations for your expected availability are much more complicated than our simple example. However, what you can take away from this is that components in series significantly increase our system's risk of experiencing downtime. You can of course mitigate this by reducing the items in series or adding multiple numbers of those components, in parallel

Rule 39—Ensure You Can Wire On and Off Functions

Rule 39: What, When, How, and Why

What: Create a framework to disable and enable features of your product.

When to use: Risky, very high use, or shared services that might otherwise cause site failures when slow to respond or unavailable.

How to use: Develop shared libraries to allow automatic or on-demand enabling and disabling of services. See Table 9.5 for recommendations.

Why: Graceful failure (or handling failures) of transactions can keep you in business while you recover from the incident and problem that caused it.

Key takeaways: Implement Wire On/Wire Off Frameworks whenever the cost of implementation is less than the risk and associated cost of failure. Work to develop shared libraries that can be reused to lower the cost of future implementation.

We introduced the notion of what we call Wire On/Wire Off frameworks in Chapter 7, "Learn from Your Mistakes," while discussing rollbacks and mentioned it again in this chapter while we were discussing fault isolation as a method of design. Ultimately these types of frameworks help to ensure that your systems can either fail gracefully (in the event of self-diagnosing frameworks) or can operate with certain functionality disabled by human intervention. Sometimes companies refer to similar functionality as *Mark Up/Mark Down* functionality or more simply enabling and disabling functionality.

There are several approaches for Wire On/Wire Off in the past, each with certain benefits and drawbacks. The approach to enabling and disabling services probably depends on the capabilities of your engineering team, your operations team, and the business criticality of the service in question. Table 9.5 covers some of these approaches.

Table 9.5 isn't meant to be an all encompassing list of the possibilities for enabling and disabling functionality. In fact, many companies blend some of these options. They may read in variables from a database or a file at startup, but also implement synchronous communication and automatic failure detection. In the case of payment gateways they may decide to automatically "auth" credit cards for some period of time, and then past a threshold of time determined by their appetite for risk, decide to just queue authorizations and move to an asynchronous method of authorization.

Table 9.5   **Wire On/Wire Off Approaches**

Approach	Description	Pro	Con
Automatic markdown based on timeouts	Useful for synchronous calls for internal and external services. Calls are not made upon markdown at all, and service is considered "offline."	Fastest way to mark down a service that might bring several other services down when slow or unavailable.	Sensitive to "false failures" or incorrect identification of a failing service. When coupled with auto markup, may cause a "pinging" effect of the service. Every service needs to make its own decision.
Stand in service	Replace a service with an auto responder with a dummy response that indicates service unavailable or a cached response of "likely good data."	Easy to implement, at least on the service side. May allow user determination of failure.	Each calling service needs to understand the "failure" response. May be slower to mark down and may require user intervention to mark up.
Synchronous markdown command	User intervention sends a command to services to stop using the failed or slow service.	Allows user determination of failed service.	Slower than automatic markdown. Also, if services have TCP ports full due to slow or failed service, the command may not work as desired. Requires user intervention to mark up.
Config file markdown	Change configuration file variable to indicate the "wire off" of a service.	Doesn't rely on request/reply communication as in a synchronous command.	Likely requires restart of a server to implement.

Approach	Description	Pro	Con
File markdown	Presence of a file (or absence of a file) indicates service up or down (can be used or not).	Doesn't rely on request/reply communication as in a synchronous command. Might not require server restart.	May slow down processes "polling" for files.
Database markdown	Use of a variable (column) per service in a database to enable or disable features.	Can be done on restart or per request. Easy to communicate to all servers by changing one location.	Requires one or more "control tables" that need to be highly available and may need to be replicated so as not to cross swimlane boundaries. If done on a transaction basis can be costly.
Runtime Variable	Read at startup as an argument to the program for daemon-like server processes.	Similar to config file.	Similar to config file.

Equally important issues to tackle when considering Wire On/Wire Off frameworks are the decisions of where and when they should be used. Clearly the work to implement the framework represents additional work and as a result additional cost to the business. Let's start with the (unlikely and probably incorrect) position that certain features would never fail. If we could tell which features would never fail, we would never want to implement this functionality for those features as it represents a cost with no return. With that starting point, we can identify where this investment has value or provides the business with a return. Any feature that has a high rate of usage (high throughput) and whose failure will impact other important features on the site is a candidate. Another candidate is any feature that is undergoing fairly significant change in a given release. The idea in both of these areas is that the cost of implementing Wire On/Wire Off is less than the risk (where risk is a function of both likelihood of a failure and the impact of that failure) to our business. If the development of a feature with this functionality is an extra $1,000 and an unhandled failure of the feature might cost us $10,000 in business is the cost justified?

When done well, engineering teams can reduce the cost of implementing a Wire On/Wire Off framework by implementing a set of shared libraries to be used across functions. This approach doesn't reduce the cost of implementing the framework to zero for any new development, but it does help to reduce the cost for future generations of framework-enabled features.

We recommend implementing Wire On/Wire Off frameworks for any shared, heavily used services such as payment gateways and computationally expensive processes such as the calculation of social network graphs. Any shared service is a shared failure point, and it is worthwhile thinking about how to work around that service should it fail. Any significant new development also carries risk equal to its development cost, and should at least be considered for such a framework. To be clear, we don't believe that everything should be capable of being enabled and disabled; such an approach is costly and ill-advised. But well run teams should be able to identify risky and shared components and implement the appropriate safeguards.

Summary

We believe that availability and scalability go hand in hand. A product that isn't highly available doesn't need to scale because users will soon stop coming. A site that can't scale won't be highly available when the demand comes because the site will be slow or completely down. Because of this you can't work on one without thinking about the other. This chapter offered four rules that help ensure your site stays highly available as well as continues to scale. Don't let a focus on scalability cause you to forget how important availability is to your customer.

10

Avoid or Distribute State

The state that we hate the most can't be found on a map of the United States or any other country for that matter. The state we hate most is persistent state (and session information) held within the application of an Internet site. And why, you might ask, do we hate state so? Session and state destroy the ultimate value promised by multitenancy within Internet (SaaS, commerce, and so on) applications. If we must keep great amounts of data associated with a user's interactions at any given time, then we can house fewer users on any given system at any given time. In the desktop world, we rarely needed to be concerned with this as we often had a lot of power and memory available for a single user at any given time. In the multitenant world, our goal is to house as many users as possible on a single system while still delivering a stellar user experience. As such, we strive to eliminate any approach that will limit the degree of tenancy on any system. State and session cost us both in terms of memory and processing power, and as a result is an enemy to our cost-effective scale goals.

While we would prefer to avoid state at all cost, it is sometimes valuable to the business. Indeed, the very nature of some applications (such as some workflow systems) requires us to model a state machine, which in turn requires some notion of state. If state is necessary, we need to implement it in a fault-tolerant, highly available, and cost-effective way such as distributing it to our end users (Rule 41) or positioning it on a special service within our infrastructure (Rule 42).

Figure 10.1 depicts, diagrammatically both our feelings on state and how to approach decisions on how to implement state.

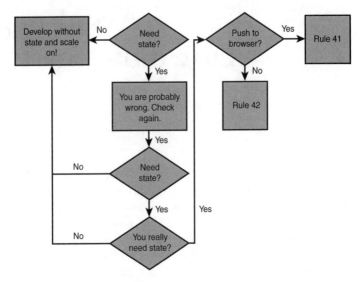

Figure 10.1   Decision flowchart for implementing state in a Web application

Rule 40—Strive for Statelessness

Rule 40: What, When, How, and Why

What: Design and implement stateless systems.

When to use: During design of new systems and redesign of existing systems.

How to use: Choose stateless implementations whenever possible. If stateful implementations are warranted for business reasons, refer to Rules 41 and 42.

Why: The implementation of state limits scalability and increases cost.

> **Key takeaways:** Always push back on the need for state in any system. Use business metrics and multivariate (or A/B) testing to determine whether state in an application truly results in the expected user behavior and business value.

Paradoxically it is both a sad and exciting day when our applications grow beyond the ability of a single server to meet the transaction processing needs of our product. It is exciting because our business is growing and sad because we embark upon a new era of development requiring new skills to scale our systems. Depending on our implementation, we can sometimes rely on clustering software with state or session replication to help us scale, but such an approach only delays the inevitable if our business continues to experience power-curve or even linear but aggressive growth. If your company is successful you will quickly grow out of this rather costly session synchronization method. As we describe in Chapter 2, "Distribute Your Work," you will soon find yourself replicating too much information in memory across too many application servers. Very likely you will need to perform a Y or Z axis split.

Many of our clients simply stop at these splits and rely on affinity maintained through a load balancer to handle session and state needs. Once a user logs in, or starts some flow specific to a pool of application servers, she maintains affinity to that application server until the function (in the case of Y axis splits where different pools provide different functions) or session (in the case of a Z axis split where customers are segmented into pools) is complete. This is an adequate approach for many products where growth has slowed or where customers have more relaxed availability requirements.

Maintaining affinity comes with some fairly high costs hinted at previously; capacity planning can become troublesome when several high volume or long running sessions become bound to a handful of servers, and availability for certain customers will be impacted when the application server on which they are running fails. While we can rely on session replication to create another host to which we might move in the event of a system failure, as described previously this approach is costly in terms of duplicated memory consumption and system capacity.

Ultimately, the solution that serves a majority of our hyper growth clients the best is to eliminate the notion of state wherever possible. We prefer to start discussions on the topic of state with "Why do you need it at all?" Our clients are often taken aback, and the typical response is "Well, that's the way it's always been and we need to know what just happened to make the next move." When pressed to back up their responses with data showing the efficacy of state in terms of revenue, increased transaction volume, and so on they are often at a loss. Granted there are certain solutions that probably need state, such as solutions that implement state machines like workflow processes. But more often than not, state is a luxury and a costly one at that.

Never underestimate the power of "simple and easy" in an application as an effective weapon against "rich and complex." Craigslist won the local classifieds war against eBay with a largely text-based and stateless application. eBay, while always attempting to stay as stateless as possible had a competing classifieds product with a significantly greater number of features and "richness" years ahead of rival Craigslist. Yet simple won the day in the local classifieds war. Not convinced? How about Google against all comers in the search market? While others invested in rich interfaces, Google at least initially built on the concept that your last search was the only thing that mattered, and what you really want is good search results. No state, no session, no nonsense.

The point is that session and state cost money and you should only implement them where there is a clear competitive advantage displayed in key operating metrics determined through A/B or multivariate analysis. Session (and state) require memory and imply greater complexity in code, which means at least slightly longer running transactions. This reduces the number of transactions we can handle per second per server, which increases the number of systems that we need. The systems may also need to be larger and more costly given the memory requirements to house state on or off the systems. Potentially we need to develop "state farms" as we describe later in this chapter, which means more devices. And of course more devices mean more space, power, and cooling or in the virtual world more cloud resources for which we are paying. Remember that every server (or virtual machine) we need costs us three times over as we need to provide space for it, cool it, and power it. Cloud resources have the same costs; they are just passed on to us in a bundle.

You are best served to have a principle that always questions the need for state in any application or service. State this principle strongly—something along the lines of "We develop stateless applications." Be clear that state distribution (the movement of state to the browser or distributed state server or cache) is not the same as stateless. Rules 41 and 42 exist to allow us to create rich business functionality where there is a clear competitive advantage, displayed through operating metrics that drive revenue and transactions, not as an alternative to this rule.

Rule 41—Maintain Sessions in the Browser When Possible

Rule 41: What, When, How, and Why

What: Try to avoid session data completely, but when needed, consider putting the data in users' browsers.

When to use: Anytime that you need session data for the best user experience.

How to use: Use cookies to store session data on the users' browsers.

Why: Keeping session data on the users' browsers allows the user request to be served by any Web server in the pool and takes the storage requirement away from your system.

Key takeaways: Using cookies to store session data is a common approach and has advantages in terms of ease of scale but also has some drawbacks. One of the most critical cons is that unsecured cookies can easily be captured and used to log into people's accounts.

If you have to keep sessions for your users, one way to do so is in the users' browsers. We'll talk about how to do this but first let's talk about the pros and cons of this approach. One benefit of putting the session data in a browser is that your system doesn't have to store the data. As we explain in Rule 42, keeping session data within the system can amount to a large overhead of storage and retrieval. Not having to do this relieves the system of a large burden in terms of storage and workload. A second benefit of this approach is that the browser's request can be serviced by any server in the pool. As you scale your Web servers along the X axis (horizontally) with the session data in the browser, any server in the pool can handle the request.

Of course since everything has its tradeoffs, one of the cons of this approach is that the data must be transferred back and forth between the browser and the servers that need this data. Moving this data back and forth for every request can be expensive, especially if the amount of data starts to become significant. Be careful not to dismiss this last statement too quickly. While your session data might not be too large now, let a couple dozen developers have access to storing data in cookies and after a couple code releases you will be wondering why the pages are loading so slowly. Another very serious con that was brought to light by the Firefox plug-in Firesheep is that session data can be easily captured on an open WiFi network and used to nefariously log in to someone else's account. With the aforementioned plug-in, session cookies from most of the popular sites such as Google, Facebook, Twitter, and Amazon, just to name a few, can be compromised. We suggest a way to protect your users' cookies against this type of hack or attack, commonly called *sidejacking*, but first let's talk about storing session data in browser cookies.

Storing cookies in browsers is simple and straightforward. In PHP, as shown in the following example, it is as simple as calling `setcookie` with the parameters of the cookie name, value, expiration, path, domain, and secure (whether it should be set only over HTTPS). To destroy the cookie when you're done with it just set the same cookie but with the expire to `time()-3600`, which sets the expiration time to one hour ago.

```
setcookie("SessionCookie", $value, time()+3600, '/', '.akf-partners.com', true);
```

Some sessions are stored in multiple cookies, and other session data is stored in a single cookie. One factor to consider is the maximum size of cookies. According to RFC2965 browsers should support cookies at least up to 4KB in size and up to 20 cookies from the same domain.[1] Most browsers, however, support these as maximums. To our earlier point, the larger the cookie the slower your pages will load since this data has to be transmitted back and forth with each request.

Now that we're using cookies to support our sessions and we're keeping them as small as possible so that our system can scale, the next question is how do we protect them from being sidejacked? Obviously you can transmit your pages and cookies all in HTTPS. The Secure Socket Layer (SSL) protocol used for HTTPS requires encrypting and decrypting all communication and requests. While this might be a requirement for a banking site, this doesn't make sense for a news or social networking site. Instead we recommend a method using at least two cookies. One cookie is an authorization cookie that is requested via HTTPS on each HTTP page using a JavaScript call such as the following. This allows the bulk of the page (content, CSS, scripts, and so on) to be transferred by unsecure HTTP but a single authorization cookie to be transferred via HTTPS.[2]

```
<script type="text/javascript" src="https://verify.akfdemo.
com/authenticate.php"></script>
```

For ultimate scalability we recommend avoiding sessions all together. However, we understand that this isn't always the case. In these cases we recommend storing the session data on the user's browser. When implementing this it is critical to maintain control of the size of the cookie data. Excessive amounts of data slow the performance of the page load as well as the Web servers on the system.

Rule 42—Make Use of a Distributed Cache for States

Rule 42: What, When, How, and Why

What: Use a distributed cache when storing session data in your system.

When to use: Anytime you need to store session data and cannot do so in users' browsers.

How to use: Watch for some common mistakes such as a session management system that requires affinity of a user to a Web server.

> **Why:** Careful consideration of how to store session data can help ensure your system will continue to scale.
>
> **Key takeaways:** Many Web servers or languages offer simple server-based session management, but these are often fraught with problems such as user affiliation with specific servers. Implementing a distributed cache allows you to store session data in your system and continue to scale.

Per our recommendations in Figure 10.1, we hope that you've taken your time in arriving at the conclusion to maintain state in your application or system and in deciding that you cannot push that state out to the end user. It is a sad, sad day that you've come this far and you should hang your head in shame that you were not enough of an engineer to figure out how to develop the system without state or without the ability to allow the end users to maintain state.

Of course we are kidding as we have already acknowledged that there are some systems that must maintain state and even a small number where that state is best maintained within the service, application, or infrastructure of your product. Granting that point, let's move on to a few rules on what *not* to do when you maintain state within your application.

First and foremost, stay away from state systems that require affinity to an application or Web server. It goes without saying that these implementations will have lower availability than those that allow remote access of state from any of a number of servers. If the server dies, all of the session information (including state) on that server will likely go away as well requiring those customers (potentially numbering into the thousands) to restart whatever process they were in. Even if you persist the data in some local or network enabled storage, the user will need to start again on another server, and there will be some interruption of service.

Second, don't use state or session replication services such as those within some application servers or third-party "clustering" servers. As stated previously in this chapter, such systems simply don't scale well as modifications to session need to be propagated to multiple nodes. Furthermore, in choosing to do this type of implementation we are creating a new concern for scalability in how much memory we use on our systems.

Third, when choosing a session or state cache or persistence engine, locate that cache away from the servers performing the actual work. While this is a bit of a nit, it does help with availability as when you lose a server you either lose the cache associated with that server or the service running on it and not both. Creating a cache (or persistent) tier also allows us to scale that tier based on the cache accesses alone rather than needing to accommodate both the application service and the internal and remote cache services.

Distributed Session/State Cache Don'ts

Here are three approaches to avoid in implementing a cache to manage session or state:

- Don't implement systems that require affinity to a server to function properly.

- Don't use state or session replication to create duplicates of data on different systems.

- Don't locate the cache on the system doing the work (this doesn't mean you shouldn't have a local application cache—just that session information is best handled in its own tier of servers).

If you abide by the rules governing what not to do, the choice of what to do becomes pretty easy. We strive to be agnostic in our approaches to such matters, and as such we care more about designs and less about the implementation details such as which open source caching or database solution you might want to implement. We do feel strongly that there is rarely a need to develop the caching solution yourself. With all of the options from distributed object caches like memcached to open source and third-party databases, it seems ludicrous that one would implement their own caching solution for session information.

This brings us to the question of what we should use for a cache. To us, the question really comes down to reliability and persistence versus cost. If you expect to keep session or state information for quite some time such as in the case of a shopping cart, you may decide that for some or all of your session information you are going to rely on a solution that allows lengthy and durable persistence. In many cases we've seen databases used for these implementations. Clearly, however, a database will cost you more per transaction than a simpler solution such as a nonpersisting distributed object cache.

If you don't need persistence and durability, you can choose from one of many object caches. Refer to Chapter 6, "Use Caching Aggressively," for a discussion on object caches and their uses. In some cases, you may decide that you want both the persistence of a database and the relative low cost for performance of a cache in front of that database. Such an implementation gives you the persistence of a database while allowing to scale the transactions more cost effectively through a cache that front ends that database.

Distributed Session/State Cache Considerations

Here are three common implementations for distributed caches and some notes on their benefits and drawbacks:

- Database-only implementations are the most costly overall, but allow all data to be persisted and handle conflicts between updates and reads very well in a distributed environment.

- Nonpersistent object caches are fast and comparatively inexpensive, but do not allow data to be recovered upon failure and aren't good for implementations with long periods between accesses by users.

- Hybrid solutions with databases providing persistency and caches providing cost-effective scale are great when persistency is required and low relative cost is preferred.

Summary

Our first recommendation is to avoid state at all cost, but we understand that session data is sometimes a necessity. If state is necessary, we first recommend trying to store the session data in the users' browsers (Rule 41). Doing so eliminates the need to store data in your system and allows for the servicing of requests by any Web server in the pool. If not possible we recommend making use of a distributed caching system for session data (Rule 42). Following these rules will help ensure your system continues to scale.

Endnotes

1. D. Kristol and L. Montulli, Networking Working Group Request for Comments 2965, "HTTP State Management Mechanism," October 2000, http://www.ietf.org/rfc/rfc2965.txt.

2. This solution was developed by Randy Wigginton, as explained and demonstrated on our blog, http://akfpartners.com/techblog/2010/11/20/slaying-firesheep/.

11

Asynchronous Communication and Message Buses

Asynchronous communication between applications and services has been both the savior and the downfall of many platforms. And the vehicle (pun intended) most often used on this journey to paradise or inferno is the message bus. When implemented properly, asynchronous communication is absolutely a valuable rung in the ladder of near infinite scale. When implemented haphazardly, it merely hides the faults and blemishes of a product and is very much akin to putting "lipstick on a pig."

As a rule, we favor asynchronous communication whenever possible. As we discuss in this chapter, this favorable treatment requires that one not only communicates in an asynchronous fashion but actually develops the application to be asynchronous in behavior. This means, in a large part, the move away from request/reply protocols—at least those with temporal constraints on responses. At the very least it requires aggressive timeouts and exception handling when responses are required within a specified period.

As the most often preferred implementation of asynchronous communication, the message bus is often underimplemented. In our experience, it is often thrown in as an afterthought without the appropriate monitoring or architectural diligence. The result is often delayed catastrophe; as critical messages back up, the system appears to be operating properly until the entire bus grinds to a halt or crashes altogether. As a critical portion of the product infrastructure, the site goes "off the air." The purpose of this chapter is to keep such brown, gray, or black-outs from happening.

Rule 43—Communicate Asynchronously As Much As Possible

Rule 43: What, When, How ,and Why

What: Use asynchronous instead of synchronous communication as often as possible.

When to use: Consider for all calls between services and tiers.

How to use: Use language specific calls to ensure the requests are made and not waited on.

Why: Synchronous calls stop the entire program's execution waiting for a response, which ties all the services and tiers together resulting in cascading failures.

Key takeaways: Use asynchronous communication techniques to ensure that each service and tier is as independent as possible. This allows the system to scale much farther than if all components are closely coupled together.

In general asynchronous calls, no matter whether they are within a service or between two different services, are much more difficult to implement than synchronous calls. The reason is that asynchronous calls often require coordination to communicate back to the service that first sent a message that the request has been completed. If you're firing and forgetting then there is no requirement for communication or coordination back to the calling method. This can easily be done a variety of ways including something as simple as the following PHP function, which makes use of the ampersand & to run the process in the background.

```
function asyncExec($filename, $options = '') {
  exec("php -f {$filename} {$options} >> /dev/null &");
}
```

However, firing and forgetting is not always an option. Often the calling method wants to know when the called method is complete. The reason for this could be that other processing has to happen before results can be returned. We can easily imagine a scenario in an ecommerce platform where the postage needs to be recalculated along with crediting discount codes. Ideally we'd like to perform these two tasks simultaneously instead of having to calculate the shipping, which might require a third-party call to a vendor, and then processing the discount codes on the items in the shopping cart. But we can't send the final results back to the user until both are complete.

In most languages there are mechanisms designed to allow for the coordination and communication between the parent method and the asynchronous child method called *callbacks*. In C/C++, this is done through function pointers; in Java, it is done through object references. There are many design patterns that use callbacks, such as the delegate design pattern and the observer design pattern. Buy why go to all this hassle to call other methods or services asynchronously?

We go through the hassle of making some of our calls asynchronously because when all the methods, services, and tiers are tied together through synchronous calls, a slow down or failure in one causes a delayed but nevertheless cascading failure in the entire system. As we discussed in Rule 38 (Chapter 9, "Design for Fault Tolerance and Graceful Failure"), putting all your components in series has a multiplicative effect of failure. We covered this concept with availability, but it also works for the risk of a bug per KLOC (thousand lines of code). If methods A, B, and C have a 99.99% chance of being bug free and one calls the other, which calls the other, all synchronously, the chance of a bug affecting that logic stream of the system is 99.99% × 99.99% × 99.99% = 99.97%.

The same concept of reducing the risk of propagating failures was covered in Rule 36 (Chapter 9). In that rule we covered the idea of splitting your system's pools into separate lanes for different sets of customers. The benefit being that if there is a problem

in one swimlane it will not propagate to the other customers'
lanes, which minimizes the impact. Additionally, fault detection
is much easier because there are multiple versions of the same
code that can be compared. This ability to more easily detect
faults when an architecture has swimlanes also applies to modules or methods that have asynchronous calls.

Asynchronous calls prevent the spreading of failures or slow-
downs, and they aid in the determination of where the bug
resides when there is a problem. Most people who have had a
database problem have seen it manifest itself in the app or Web
tier because a slow query causes connections to back up and
then sockets to remain open on the app server. The database
monitoring might not complain, but the application monitoring
will. In this case you have synchronous calls between the app
and database servers, and the problem becomes more difficult to
diagnose.

Of course you can't have all asynchronous calls between
methods and tiers in your system, so the real question is which
ones should be made asynchronous. To start with calls that are
not asynchronous should have timeouts that allow for gracefully
handling errors or continued processing when a synchronously
called method or service fails. The way to determine which calls
are asynchronous candidates is to analyze each call based on the
criteria such as the following:

- **External API/third party**—Is the call to a third party or
  external API? If so these absolutely should be made into
  asynchronous calls. Way too many things can go wrong
  with external calls to make these synchronous. If any way
  possible, you do not want the health and availability of
  your system tied to a system that you can't control.

- **Long running processes**—Is the process being called
  notorious for being long running? Are the computational
  or I/O requirements significant? If so these calls are great
  candidates for asynchronous calls. Often the more problematic issues are with slow running processes rather than
  outright failures.

- **Error prone/changed frequently methods**—Is the call to a method that gets changed frequently? The greater the number of changes the more likely there is to be a bug within the code. Avoid tying critical code with code that needs to be changed frequently. That is asking for an increased number of failures.

- **Temporal constraint**—When there does not exist a temporal constraint between two processes consider firing and forgetting the child process. This might be the scenario when a new registrant receives a welcome e-mail. While your system should care if the e-mail doesn't go out, the results of the registration page back to the user should not be stalled waiting for it to be sent.

These are just a few of the most important criteria to use in determining whether a call should be made asynchronously. A full set of considerations is left as an exercise for the reader and the reader's team. While we could list out another ten of these criteria as we increase in numbers they become more specific to particular systems. Also, going through the exercise with your team of developers for an hour will make everyone aware of the pros and cons of using synchronous and asynchronous calls, which is more powerful in terms of following this rule and thus scaling your systems than any list that we could provide.

Rule 44—Ensure Your Message Bus Can Scale

Rule 44: What, When, How, and Why

What: Message buses can fail from demand like any other physical or logical system. They need to be scaled.

When to use: Anytime a message bus is part of your architecture.

How to use: Employ the Y and Z AKF Axes of Scale.

Why: To ensure your bus scales to demand.

Key takeaways: Treat message buses like any other critical component of your system. Scale them ahead of demand using either the Y or Z axes of scale.

One of the most common failures we identify within technology architectures is a giant single point of failure often dubbed
the *enterprise service bus* or message bus. While the former is typically a message bus on steroids that often includes transformation
capabilities and interaction APIs, it is also more likely to have
been implemented as a single artery through the technology
stack replete with aged messages clinging to its walls like so
much cholesterol. When asked, our clients most often claim the
asynchronous nature of messages transiting this bus as a reason
why time wasn't spent on splitting up the bus to make it more
scalable or highly available. While it is true that applications
designed to be asynchronous are often more resilient to failure,
and while these apps also tend to scale more efficiently, they are
still prone to high demand bottlenecks and failure points. The
good news is that the principles you have learned so far in this
book will as easily resolve the scalability needs of a message bus
as they will solve the needs of a database.

Asynchronous systems tend to scale more easily and tend to
be more highly available than synchronous systems. This attribute
is due in a large part to the component systems and services
being capable of continuing to function in the absence or tardi-
ness of certain data. But these systems still need to offload and
accept information to function. When the system or service that
allows them to "fire and forget" or to communicate but not
block on a response becomes slow or unavailable, they are still
subject to the problems of having logical ports fill up to the
point of system failure. Such failures are absolutely possible in
message buses, as the "flesh and blood" of these systems is still
the software and hardware that run any other system. While
in some cases the computational logic that runs the bus is distributed among several servers, systems and software are still
required to allow the passing and interpretation of messages
sent over the bus.

Having dispelled the notion that message buses somehow
defy the laws of physics that bind the rest of our engineering
endeavors, we can move on to how to scale them. We know
that one of anything, whether it is physical or logical, is a bad

idea from both an availability and scalability perspective, so we need to split it up. As you may have already surmised from our previous hint, a good approach is to apply the AKF Scale Cube to the bus. In this particular case, though, we can remove the X axis of scale (see Rule 7, Chapter 2, "Distribute Your Work") as cloning the bus probably won't buy us much. By simply duplicating the bus infrastructure and the messages transiting the bus we would potentially raise our availability (one bus fails, the other could continue to function), but we would still be left with a scale problem. Potentially we could send 1/Nth the messages on each of the N buses that we implement, but then all potential applications would need to listen to all buses. We still potentially have a reader congestion problem. What we need is a way to separate or differentiate our messages by something unique to the message or data (the Y axis—Rule 8, Chapter 2) or something unique to the customer or user (the Z axis—Rule 9, Chapter 2). Figure 11.1 is a depiction of the AKF's Three Axes of Scale repurposed to message queues.

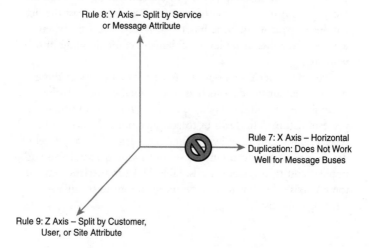

Figure 11.1   AKF Scale Cube for message buses

Having discarded the X axis of scale, let's further investigate
the Y axis of scale. There are several ways in which we might
discriminate or separate messages by attribute. One easy way is
to dedicate buses to particular purposes. For a commerce site, we
may choose a resource-oriented approach that transits customer
data on one bus (or buses), catalog data on another, purchase
data on another, and so on. We may also chose a services-
oriented approach and identify affinity relationships between
services and implement buses unique to affinity groups. "Hold
on," you cry, "if we choose such an approach of segmentation,
we lose some of the flexibility associated with buses. We can't
simply hook up some new service capable of reacting to all
messages and adding new value in our product."

    The answer, of course, is that you are absolutely correct. Just
as the splitting of databases reduces the flexibility associated with
having all of your data comingled in a single place for future
activity, so does the splitting of a service bus reduce flexibility in
communication. But remember that these splits are to enable the
greater good of enabling hyper growth and staying in business!
Do you want to have a flat business that can't grow past the limitations of your monolithic bus, or be wildly successful when
exponentially increasing levels of demand come flooding into
your site?

    We have other Y axis options as well. We can look at things
we know about the data such as its temporal qualities. Is the data
likely to be needed quickly or is it just a "for your information"
piece of datum? This leads us to considerations of quality of
service, and segmenting by required service level for any level of
data means that we can build buses of varying quality levels and
implied cost to meet our needs. Table 11.1 summarizes some of
these Y axis splits, but it is by no means meant to be an all-
encompassing list.

Table 11.1   **AKF Y Axis Splits of Message Bus**

Attribute Split	Pro	Con
Temporal	Monitoring for failures to meet response times is easy—just look for the oldest message against an absolute standard.	Not all messages are created equal. Some may be small and fast but not necessary for critical function completion.
Service	Only connects systems that need to communicate with each other.	Reduction in flexibility with various nodes connected in affinity fashion.
Quality of service	Costs to scale and make any bus highly available can scale in accordance with the importance of the message.	Likely to still need a way to scale buses with a lot of traffic for either highly important or unimportant messages.
Resource	Similar types of data (rather than the services) share a bus. Simple logical implementation.	May require some services to listen for infrequent messages on a bus.

Returning to Figure 11.1, we now apply the AKF Z axis of scale to our problem. As previously identified this approach is most often implemented by splitting buses by customer. It makes most sense when your implementation has already employed a Z axis split, as each of the swimlanes or pods can have a dedicated message bus. In fact, this would need to be the case if we truly wanted fault isolation (see Chapter 9). That doesn't mean that we can't leverage one or more message buses to communicate asynchronously between swimlanes. But we absolutely do not want to rely on a single shared infrastructure among the swimlanes for transactions that should complete within the swimlane.

The most important point in determining how to scale a message bus is to ensure that the approach is consistent with the approach applied to the rest of the technology architecture. If, for instance, you have scaled your architecture along customer

boundaries using the AKF Z axis of scale then it makes most
sense to put a message bus in each of these pods of customers. If
you have split up functions or resources as in the Y axis of scale,
then it makes sense that the message buses should follow a similar trend. If you have done both Y and Z axis and need only one
method for the amount of message traffic you experience, the Z
axis should most likely trump the Y axis to allow for greater
fault isolation.

Rule 45—Avoid Overcrowding Your Message Bus

Rule 45: What, When, How, and Why

What: Limit bus traffic to items of higher value than the cost to
handle them.

When to use: On any message bus.

How to use: Value and cost justify message traffic. Eliminate low
value, high cost traffic. Sample low value/low cost and high
value/high cost traffic to reduce the cost.

Why: Message traffic isn't "free" and presents costly demand on
your system.

Key takeaways: Don't publish everything. Sample traffic to
ensure alignment between cost and value.

Nearly anything, if done to excess, can have severe and negative
consequences. Physical fitness, for example, if taken to an extreme
over long periods of time can actually depress the immune system of the body and leave the person susceptible to viruses. Such
is the case with publishing absolutely everything that happens
within your product on one (or if you follow Rule 43—several)
message buses. The trick is to know which messages have value,
determine how much value they have, and determine whether
that value is worth the cost of publishing the message at volume.

Why, having just explained how to scale a message bus, are
we so interested in how much information we send to this now
nearly infinitely scalable system? The answer is the cost and
complexity of our scalable solution. While we are confident that

following the advice in Rule 42 will result in a scalable solution, we want that solution to scale within certain cost constraints. We often see our clients publishing messages for nearly every action taken by every service. In many cases, this publication of information is duplicative of data that their application also stores in some log file locally (as in a Web log). Very often they will claim that the data is useful in troubleshooting problems or in identifying capacity bottlenecks (even while it may actually create some of those bottlenecks). In one case we've even had a client claim that we were the reason they published everything on the bus! This client claimed that they took our advice of "Design your systems to be monitored" (See Rule 49 in Chapter 12, "Miscellaneous Rules") to mean "Capture everything your system does."

Let's start with the notion that not all data has equivalent value to your business. Clearly in a for-profit business, the data that is necessary to complete revenue producing transactions is more important in most cases than data that helps us analyze transactions for future actions. Data that helps us get smarter about what we do in the future is probably more important than data that helps us identify bottlenecks (although the latter is absolutely very important). Clearly most data has some "option value" in that we might find use for it later, but this value is lower than the value of data that has a clear and meaningful impact on our business today. In some cases, having a little bit of data gives us nearly as much value as having all of it as in the case of statistically significant sampling of lower value data in a high transaction system.

In most systems and especially across most message buses (except when we segment by quality of service in Rule 44) data has a somewhat consistent cost. Even though the value of a transaction or data element (datum) may change by the type of transaction or even value of the customer, the cost of handling that transaction remains constant. This runs counter to how we want things to work. Ideally we want the value of any element of our system to significantly exceed the cost of that element or in the worst case do no more than equal the cost. Figure 11.2 shows a simple illustration of this relationship and explains the actions a team should take with regard to the data.

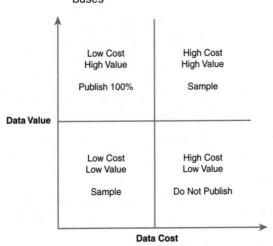

Figure 11.2   Cost/value relationship of data
and corresponding message bus action

The upper-left quadrant of Figure 11.2 is the best possible case—a case where the value of the data far exceeds the cost of sending it across the bus. In commerce sites clear examples of these transactions would be shopping cart transactions. The lower-right quadrant is an area in which we probably just discard the data altogether. A potential case might be where someone changes his profile picture on a social networking site (assuming that the profile picture change actually took place without a message being produced).

The rate at which we publish something has an impact on its cost on the message bus. As we increase the demand on the bus, we increase the cost of the bus(es) as we need to scale it to meet the new demand. Sampling allows us to reduce the cost of those transactions, and in some cases as we've described previously may still allow us to retain 100% of the value of those transactions. The act of sampling serves to reduce the cost of the transaction and move us from right to left and may allow us to get the value of the data to exceed the cost thereby allowing us to keep some portion of the data. Reducing the cost of the transaction means we can reduce the size and complexity of our message bus(es) as we reduce the total number of messages being sent.

The overall message here is that just because you have implemented a message bus doesn't mean that you have to use it for everything. There will be a strong urge to send more messages than are necessary, and you should fight that urge. Always remember that not every datum is created equally in terms of value, while its cost is likely equal to that of its peers. Use the technique of sampling to reduce the cost of handling data, and throw away (or do not publish) those things of low value. We return to the notion of value and cost in Rule 47 (Chapter 12) when we discuss storage.

Summary

This chapter is about asynchronous communication, and while it is the preferred method of communication it is generally more difficult, more expensive (in terms of development and system costs), and can actually be done to excess. We started this chapter by providing an overview of asynchronous communication and then offering a few of the most critical guidelines for when to implement asynchronous communication. We then followed up with two rules dealing with message buses, which are one of the most popular implementations of asynchronous communication.

In Rules 43 and 44, we covered how to scale a message bus and how to avoid overcrowding it. As we mentioned in the introduction to this chapter the message bus, while often the preferred implementation of asynchronous communication, is also often underimplemented. Being thrown in as an afterthought without the appropriate monitoring or architectural diligence, this can turn out to be a huge nightmare instead of an architectural advantage.

Pay attention to these rules to ensure that the communication within and between services can scale effectively as your system grows.

12

Miscellaneous Rules

We're not going to lie to you—we ran out of themes and catchy titles for the rules in this chapter. But even without a theme these rules are important. Two of these rules deal with the competencies of your team; one cautions you not to over-rely on third-party solutions for scale, and the other urges you to build the necessary competencies to be world class for each portion of your technology architecture and infrastructure. One rule outlines the foolishness of relying on stored procedures for business logic, including the hazards to scale and long-term costs to your company. Yet another rule examines the need for products to be designed from day one with monitoring in mind.

Rule 46—Be Wary of Scaling Through Third Parties

Rule 46: What, When, How, and Why

What: Scale your own system; don't rely on vendor solutions to achieve scalability.

When to use: Whenever considering whether to use a new feature or product from a vendor.

How to use: Rely on the rules of this book for understanding how to scale and use vendor provided products and services in the most simplistic manner possible.

Why: Three reasons for following this rule: Own your destiny, keep your architecture simple, and reduce your total cost of ownership.

> **Key takeaways:** Do not rely on vendor products, services, or features to scale your system. Keep your architecture simple, keep your destiny in your own hands, and keep your costs in control. All three of these can be violated by using a vendor's proprietary scaling solution.

As you climb the management track in technology organizations you invariably start to attend vendor meetings and eventually get solicited by vendors almost constantly. In a world where global IT spending of over $781 billion fell 6.9% in 2009,[1] you can safely bet that vendors are recruiting the best salespeople possible and are working their hardest to sell you their products and services. These vendors are often sophisticated in their approaches and truly consider it a long-term relationship with clients. Unfortunately, this long-term relationship is actively managed for the clients to end up spending more and more with the vendor. This is all great business and we don't fault the vendors for trying, but we do want to caution you as a technologist or business leader to be aware of the pros and cons of relying on vendors to help you scale. We're going to cover three reasons that you should avoid relying on vendors to scale.

First, we believe that you should want the fate of your company, your team, and your career in your own hands. Looking for vendors to relieve you of this burden will likely result in a poor outcome because to the vendor you're just one of many customers so they are not going to respond to your crisis like you will respond. As a CTO or technology leader, if the vendor you vetted and selected fails, causing downtime for your business, you are just as responsible as if you had written every line of code. All code has bugs, even vendor provided code, and if you don't believe this ask the vendor for how many patches they've produced for a specific version. Just like all code the patches are 99% bug fixes with the major versions reserved for new features. We would rather have the source code to fix a problem than have to rely on a vendor to find the problem and provide you with a patch, which often takes days if it ever occurs. This should not be taken to imply that you should do everything yourself such as writing your own database or firewall. Use vendors for things that they can do better than you and that are not part of your core competency. Ultimately we are talking about ensuring that you can split up your application and product to allow it to scale as scaling should be a core competency of yours.

Second, with scalability, as with most things in life, simple is better. We teach a simple cube (see Chapter 2, "Distribute Your Work") to understand how to build scalable architectures. The more complex you make your system the more you are likely to suffer from availability issues. More complex systems are more difficult and more costly to maintain. Clustering technologies are much more complex than straightforward log shipping for creating read replicas. Recall Rules 1 and 3 from this book: Do not overengineer the solution and simplify the solution three times over.

Third, let's talk about the real total cost of trying to scale with vendors. One of our architectural principles, and should be one of yours as well, is that the most cost-effective way to scale is to be vendor neutral. Locking yourself into a single vendor gives them the upper hand in negotiations. We're going to pick on database vendors for a bit, but this discussion applies to almost all technology vendors. The reason database companies build additional features into their systems is that their revenue streams faster than just the adoption of new customers would normally allow. The way to achieve this is through a technique called up-selling and involves getting existing customers to purchase more or additional features or services.

One of the most prevalent add-on features for databases is clustering. It's a perfect feature in that it supposedly solves a problem that customers who are growing rapidly need solving—scalability of the customer's platform. Additionally, it is proprietary, meaning that once you start using one vendor's clustering service you can't just switch to another's solution. If you're a CTO of a hyper growth company that needs to continue producing new features for your customers and might not be that familiar with scaling architectures, when a vendor waltzes in and tells you that they have a solution to your biggest, scariest problem, you're anxious to jump on board with them. And, often the vendor will make the jump very easy by throwing in this additional feature for the first year contract. The reason they do this is that they know this is the hook. If you start scaling with their technology solution you'll be reluctant to switch, and they can increase prices dramatically with you having very few alternatives.

For these three reasons, control of your own destiny, additional complexity, and total cost of ownership, we implore you to consider scaling without relying on vendors. The rules in this book should more than adequately arm you and your team with the knowledge to get started scaling in a simple but effective manner.

Rule 47—Purge, Archive, and Cost-Justify Storage

Rule 47: What, When, How, and Why

What: Match storage cost to data value, including removing data of value lower than the costs to store it.

When to use: Apply to data and its underlying storage infrastructure during design discussions and throughout the lifecycle of the data in question.

How to use: Apply recency, frequency, and monetization analysis to determine the value of the data. Match storage costs to data value.

Why: Not all data is created equal (that is, of the same value), and in fact it often changes in value over time. Why then should we have a single storage solution with equivalent cost for that data?

Key takeaways: It is important to understand and calculate the value of your data and to match storage costs to that value. Don't pay for data that doesn't have a stakeholder return.

Storage has been getting cheaper, faster, and denser just as processors have been getting faster and cheaper. As a result, some companies and many organizations within companies just assume that storage is virtually free. In fact, a marketing professional asked us in 2002 why we were implementing mail file size maximum constraints while companies like Google and Yahoo! were touting free unlimited personal e-mail products. Our answer was twofold and forms the basis for this rule. First, the companies offering these solutions expected to make money off their products through advertising, whereas it was unclear how much additional revenue the marketing person was committing to while asking for more storage. Second, and most importantly, while the marketing professional considered a decrease in cost to be virtually "free," the storage in fact still costs money in at least three ways: The storage itself costs money to purchase, the space it occupied costs us money (or lost opportunity relative to high-er value services where we owned the space), and the power and HVAC to spin and cool the drives was increasing rather than decreasing in cost on a per-unit basis.

Discussing this point with our marketing colleague, we came upon a shared realization and a solution to the problem. The realization was that not every piece of data (or e-mail), whether it be used for a product or to run an IT back office system, is of equivalent value. We hinted at this concept in Chapter 11, "Asynchronous Communication and Message Buses," Rule 44, while discussing message buses and asynchronous communica-tion. Order history in commerce systems provides a great exam-ple of this concept; the older the data the less meaningful it is to our business and our customer. Our customers aren't likely to go back and view purchase data that is ten years, five years, or possi-bly even two years old, and even if they are the frequency of that viewing is likely to decay over time. Furthermore, that data isn't likely as meaningful to our business in determining product rec-ommendations as more recent purchase information (except in the case of certain durable goods that get replaced in those intervals like vehicles). Given this reduction in value both to the customer and to our business, why would we possibly want to store it on systems that cost us the same as more recent data?

The solution was to apply a marketing concept known as RFM, which stands for *recency, frequency, and monetization* analysis. Marketing gurus use this technique to make recommendations to people or send special offers to keep high value customers happy or to "reactivate" those who haven't been active recently. The concept is extensible to our storage needs (or as the case may be our storage woes). Many of our clients tell us that the largest growing portion of their budget and in some cases the largest single component of their budget is storage. We've applied this RFM technique within their businesses to help both mature their understanding of the data residing on their storage subsystems and ultimately solve the problem through a tiered storage archival and purge strategy.

First we need an understanding of the meaning of the terms within RFM analysis. *Recency* accounts for how recently the data item in question has been accessed. This might be a file in your storage system or rows within a database. *Frequency* speaks to how frequently that data is accessed. Sometimes this is captured as the mean period between access and the rough inverse of this—the number of accesses over some time interval. Monetization is the value that a specific piece of data has to your business in general. When applied to data, these three terms help us calculate overall business value and access speeds. As you might expect, we are moving toward applying our proprietary cube to yet another problem! By matching the type of storage to the value of the data in an RFM-like approach, we might have a cube that has high cost storage mapped to high value data in the upper right and an approach to delete and/or archive data in the bottom left. The resulting cube is shown in Figure 12.1.

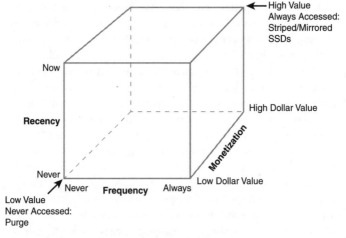

Figure 12.1   AKF Scale Cube applied to RFM
storage analysis

The X axis of our repurposed cube addresses the frequency of access. The axis moves from data that is "never" (or very infrequently) accessed to that which is accessed constantly or always. The Y axis of the cube identifies recency of access and has low values of never to high values of the data being accessed right now. The Z axis of the cube deals with monetization, from values of no value to very high value. Using the cube as a method of analysis, one could plot potential solutions along the multiple dimensions of the cube. Data in the lower left and front portion of the cube has no value and was never accessed, meaning that we should purge this data if regulatory conditions allow us to do so. Why would we incur a cost for data that won't return value to our business? The upper right and back portion of our three-dimensional cube identifies the most valuable pieces of business data. We strive to store these on the solutions with the highest reliability and fastest access times such that the transactions that use them can happen quickly for our clients. Ideally we would cache this data somewhere as well as having it on a stable storage solution, but the underlying storage solution might be the fastest solid state disks that current technology supports. These disks might be striped and mirrored for access speed and high availability.

The product of our RFM analysis might yield a score for the value of the data overall. Maybe it's as simple as a product or maybe you'll add some magic of your own that actually applies some dollar value to the resulting score. If we employed this dollar value score to a value curve that matched the resulting RFM value to the cost of a solution to support it we might end up with a diagram similar to that of Figure 12.2.

We purge very low value data, just as we did in our analysis of the cube of Figure 12.1. Low value data goes on low cost systems with slow access times. If you need to access it, you can always do it offline and e-mail a report or whatever to the requester. High value systems might go on very fast but relatively costly SSDs or some storage area network equivalent. The curve of Figure 12.2 is purely illustrative and was not developed with actual data. Because data varies in value across businesses, and because the cost of the solutions to support this data change over time, you should develop your own solution. Some data might need to be kept for some period of time due to regulatory or legal reasons. In these cases we look to put the data on the cheapest solution possible to meet our legal/regulatory requirements while not making the data dilutive in terms of shareholder value.

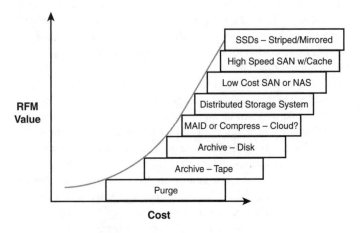

Figure 12.2   RFM value, cost, and
solution curve

It is important to keep in mind that data ages, and the RFM cube recognizes this fact. As a result, it isn't a one-time analysis but rather a living process. As datum ages and decays in value, so too do we want to move it to storage cost consistent with that declining value. As such, we need to have processes and procedures to "archive" data or to move it to lower cost systems. In rare cases, data may actually increase in value with age and so we may also need systems to move data to higher cost (more reliable and faster) storage over time. Make sure you address these needs in your architecture.

Rule 48—Remove Business Intelligence from Transaction Processing

> ### Rule 48: What, When, How, and Why
>
> **What:** Separate business systems from product systems and product intelligence from database systems.
>
> **When to use:** Anytime you are considering internal company needs and data transfer within, to, or from your product.
>
> **How to use:** Remove stored procedures from the database and put them in your application logic. Do not make synchronous calls between corporate and product systems.
>
> **Why:** Putting application logic in databases is costly and represents scale challenges. Tying corporate systems and product systems together is also costly and represents similar scale challenges as well as availability concerns.
>
> **Key takeaways:** Databases and internal corporate systems can be costly to scale due to license and unique system characteristics. As such, we want them dedicated to their specific tasks. In the case of databases, we want them focused on transactions rather than product intelligence. In the case of back office systems (business intelligence), we do not want our product tied to their capabilities to scale. Use asynchronous transfer of data for business systems.

We often tell our clients to steer clear of stored procedures within in relational databases. One of their first questions is typically "Why do you hate stored procedures so much?" The truth is that we don't dislike stored procedures. In fact, we've used them with great effect on many occasions. The problem is that stored procedures are often overused within solutions, and this overuse sometimes causes scalability bottlenecks in systems that would otherwise scale efficiently and almost always results in a very high cost of scale. Given the emphasis on databases, why didn't we put this rule in the chapter on databases? The answer is that the drivers of our concerns over stored procedures are really driven by the need to separate business intelligence and product intelligence from transaction processing. In general, this concept can be further abstracted to "Keep like transactions together (or alternatively separate unlike transactions) for the highest possible availability and scalability and best possible cost." Those are a lot of words for a principle, so let's first return to our concern over stored procedures and databases as an illustration as to why this separation should occur.

Databases tend to be one of the most expensive systems or services within your architecture. Even in the case where you are using an open source database, in most cases the servers upon which these systems exist are attached to a relatively high cost storage solution (compared to other solutions you might own), have the fastest and largest number of processors, and have the greatest amount of memory. Often, in mature environments, these systems are tuned to do one thing well—perform relational operations and commit transactions to a stable storage engine as quickly as possible. The cost per compute cycle on these systems tends to be higher than the remainder of the solutions or services within a product's architecture (for example, application servers or Web servers). These systems also tend to be the points at which certain services converge and the defining points for a swimlane. In the most extreme sense, such as in a young product, they might be monolithic in nature and as a result the clear governor of scale for the environment.

For all these reasons, using this expensive compute resource for business logic makes very little sense. Each transaction will only cost us more as the system is more expensive to operate. The system is likely also a governor to our scale, so why would we want to steal capacity by running other than relational transactions on it? For all these reasons, we should limit these systems to database (or storage related or NoSQL) transactions to allow the systems to do what they do best. In so doing we can both increase our scalability and reduce our cost for scale.

Using the database as a metaphor, we can apply this separation of dissimilar services to other pieces of our architecture. We very likely have back office systems that perform functions like e-mail sending and receiving (nonplatform related), general ledger and other accounting activities, marketing segmentation, customer support operations, and so on. In each of these cases, we may be enticed to simply bolt these things onto our platform. Perhaps we want a transaction purchased in our ecommerce system to immediately show up in our CFO's Enterprise Resource Planning system. Or maybe we want it to be immediately available to our customer support representatives in case something goes wrong with the transaction. Similarly, if we are running an advertising platform we might want to analyze data from our data warehouse in real time to suggest even better advertising. There are a number of reasons why we might want to mix our business process related systems with our product platform. We have a simple answer: Don't do it.

Ideally we want these systems to scale independently relative to their individual needs. By tying these systems together, each of them needs to scale at the same rate as the system making requests of them. In some cases, as was the case with our database performing business logic, the systems may be more costly to scale. This is often the case with ERP systems that have licenses associated with CPUs to run them. Why would we possibly want to increase our cost of scale by making a synchronous call to the ERP system for each transaction? Moreover, why would we want to reduce the availability of our product platform by adding yet another system in series as we discussed in Chapter 9, "Design for Fault Tolerance and Graceful Failure," Rule 38?

Just as product intelligence should not be placed on databases, business intelligence should not be tied to product transactions. There are many cases where we need that data resident within our product, and in those cases we should do just that—make it resident within the product. We can select data sets from these other systems and represent them appropriately within our product offering. Often this data will be best served with a new or different representation—sometimes of a different normal form. Very often we need to move data from our product back to our business systems such as in the case of customer support systems, marketing systems, data warehouses, and ERP systems. In these cases, we will also likely want to summarize and/or represent the data differently. Furthermore, to increase our availability we will want these pieces of data moved asynchronously back and forth between the systems. ETL, or extract, transform, and load, systems are widely available for such purposes, and there are even open source tools available to allow you to build your own ETL processes.

And remember that asynchronous does not mean "old" or "stale" data. There is little reason why you can select elements of data over small time periods and move them around between systems. Additionally, you can always publish the data on some sort of message bus for use on these other systems. The lowest cost solution will be batch extraction, but if temporal constraints don't allow such cost-efficient movement then message buses are absolutely an appropriate solution. Just remember to revisit our rules on message buses and asynchronous transactions in Chapter 11.

Rule 49—Design Your Application to Be Monitored

Rule 49: What, When, How, and Why

What: Think about how you will need to monitor your application as you are designing it.

When to use: Anytime you add or change modules of your code base.

How to use: Build hooks into your system to record transaction times.

Why: Having insight into how your application is performing will help answer many questions when there is a problem.

Key takeaways: Adopt as an architectural principle that your application must be monitored. Additionally, look at your overall monitoring strategy to make sure you are first answering the question of "Is there a problem?" and then the "Where" and "What."

When it comes to monitoring, most SaaS companies start by installing one of the open source monitoring tools such as Cacti, Ntop, or Nagios, just to name a few. This is a great way to check in on network traffic or the servers' CPU and memory but requires someone to pay attention to the monitors. The next step for most companies is to set up an automatic alerting system, which is a nice step forward. The problem with this scenario is that if you follow these steps by now you're at a point where you are paging out at least one person in the middle of the night when a server starts consuming too much memory. If your reaction is "great!" then let me ask the question "Is there a problem with your site?" The reality is that you don't know.

Just because a server has a high CPU or memory utilization does not mean that your customers are having any issue with your site at all. And while reacting to every bump in the night on your system is better than ignoring them, the best solution is to actually know the impact of that bump on your customers to determine the most appropriate response. The way to achieve this is to monitor your system from the perspective of a business metric. For example, if you have an ecommerce site you might want to monitor the number of items put into shopping carts or the total value of purchases per time period (sec, minute, 10 mins, and so on). For an auction site you might want to monitor the number of items listed or the number of searches performed per time period. The correct time period is the one that smoothes out the data points enough that the normal variation doesn't obscure real issues. When you plot these business metrics on a graph against the data from a week ago (week-over-week) you can start to easily see when there is a problem.

Figure 12.3 shows a graph of new account signups for a site. The solid line represents data from last week, and the dotted line represents data from this week. Notice the drop starting around 9:00 a.m. and lasting until 3:00 p.m. From this graph it is obvious that there was a problem. If the cause of this problem had been a network issue with your ISP, monitoring your servers would not have caught this. Their CPU and memory would have been fine during these six hours because very little processing was taking place on them. The next step after plotting this data is to put an automated check that compares today's values against last week's and alerts when it is out of statistical significance.[2]

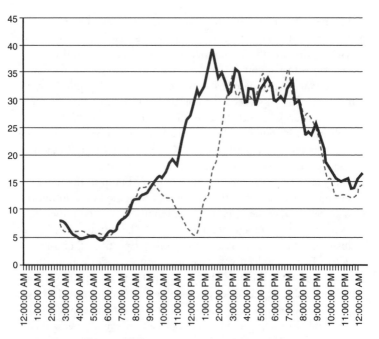

Figure 12.3   Monitoring business metrics

Once you know there is a problem affecting your customers, you can react appropriately and start asking the other questions that monitoring is designed to answer. These questions include "Where is the problem?" and "What is the problem?" Figure 12.4 shows two triangles. The one on the left represents the scope of the question being asked, and the one on the right represents how much data is required to answer that question. Answering the question "Is there a problem?" doesn't require much data but is very large in terms of scope. This as we previously discussed is best answered by monitoring business metrics. The next question "Where is the problem?" requires more data, but the scope is smaller. This is the level at which monitoring of the application will help answer this question. We cover this in more detail later in the chapter. The last question "What is the problem?" requires the most data but is the most narrow in scope. This is where the Nagios, Cacti, and so on can be used to answer the question.

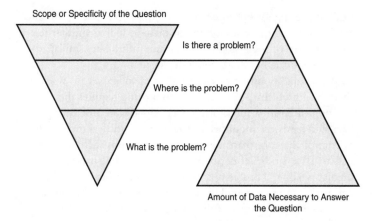

Figure 12.4   Monitoring scope versus amount
of data

Rule 16 covered the importance of trapping exceptions, logging
them, and monitoring the logs. We're going to expand on the
concept by discussing how you not only should catch errors and
exceptions but also should adopt as an architectural principle the
concept of "design to be monitored." This simply stated is the
idea that your application code should make it easy to place
hooks in for watching the execution of transactions such as
SQL, API, RPC, or method calls. Some of the best monitored
systems have asynchronous calls before and after a transaction to
record the start time, transaction type, and end time. These are
then posted on a bus or queue to be processed by a monitoring
system. Tracking and plotting this data can yield all types of
insights into answering the question of "Where is the problem?"

Once you've mastered answering these three questions of "Is
there a problem?"; "Where is the problem?"; and "What is the
problem?" there are a couple of advanced monitoring questions
that you can start to ask. The first is "Why is there a problem?"
This question usually gets asked during the postmortem process
as discussed in Rule 30. When performing continuous deploy-
ments, answering this problem requires a much faster cycle than
a typical postmortem. Your organization must integrate learning

from answering "Why" into the next hour's code release. Insights from answering this question might include adding another test to the smoke or regression test to ensure future bugs similar to this one get caught before being deployed.

A final question that monitoring can help answer is "Will there be a problem?" This type of monitoring requires the combination of business monitoring data, application monitoring data, and hardware monitoring data. Using statistical tools such as control charts or machine learning algorithms such as neural nets or Bayesian belief networks, this data can be analyzed to predict whether a problem is likely to occur. A final step to this and perhaps the holy grail of monitoring would be for the system to take action when it thinks a problem will occur and fix itself. Considering that today most automatic failover monitors mess up and failover inappropriately we know automatic or self-healing systems are a long way off.

While predicting problems sounds like a fun computer science project, don't even think about it until you have all the other steps of monitoring in place and working well. Start monitoring from the customer's perspective by using business metrics. This will start you off on the appropriate level of response to all the other monitoring.

Rule 50—Be Competent

Rule 50: What, When, How, and Why

What: Be competent, or buy competency in/for each component of your architecture.

When to use: For any Internet service or commerce solution.

How to use: For each component of your infrastructure, identify the team responsible and level of competency with that component.

Why: To a customer, every problem is *your* problem. You can't blame suppliers or providers. You provide a service—not software.

Key takeaways: Don't confuse competence with build versus buy or core versus context decisions. You can buy solutions and still be competent in their deployment and maintenance. In fact, your customers demand that you do so.

Maybe you think that this particular rule goes without saying. "Of course we are competent in what we do—how else could we remain in business?" For the purpose of this rule, we are going to assume that you have an Internet offering—some sort of SaaS platform, ecommerce offering, or some other solution delivered over the Internet.

How well does your team really understand the load balancers that you use? How often are you required to get outside help to resolve problems or figure out how to implement something on those load balancers? What about your databases? Do your developers or DBAs know how to identify which tables need indices and which queries are running slowly? Do you know how to move tables around on file systems to reduce contention and increase overall capacity? How about your application servers? Who is your expert with those?

Perhaps your answer to all these questions is that you don't really need to do those things. Maybe you've read books, including at least one other that these authors have written, that indicate you should identify the things in which you have value producing differentiation capabilities and specialize in those areas. The decision that something is "non-core" or that one should buy versus build (as in the case of a build versus buy decision) should not be confused with whether your team should be competent in the technology that you buy. It absolutely makes sense for you to use a third-party or open source database, but that doesn't mean that you don't have to understand and be capable of operating and troubleshooting that database.

Your customers expect you to deliver a service to them. To that end, the development of unique software to create that service is a means to an end. You are, at the end of the day, in the service business. Make no mistake about that. It is a mindset requirement that when not met has resulted in the deterioration and even death of companies. Friendster's focus on the "F-graph," the complex solution that calculated relationships within the social network, was at least one of the reasons Facebook won the private social network race. At the heart of this focus was an attitude held within many software shops—a focus that the challenging problem of the F-graph needed to be solved. This focus led to a number of outages within the site, or very slow response times as systems ground to a halt while attempting to compute relationships in near real time. Contrast this with a focus on a service, where availability and response time are more important than any particular feature. Software is just a means for providing that service.

But in our world you also need more than just software. Infrastructure is also important to help us get transactions processed on time and in a highly available manner. Just as we might focus too much on the solution to a single problem, so might we overlook the other components within our architecture that deliver that service. If we must be competent in our software to deliver a service, so must we be competent in everything else that we employ to deliver that service. Our customers expect superior service delivery. They don't understand and don't care that you didn't develop and aren't an expert in the particular component of your architecture that is failing.

So it is that while we don't need to develop every piece of our solution (in fact we should not develop every piece), we do need to understand each piece. For anything we employ, we need to know that we are using it correctly, maintaining it properly, and restoring it to service promptly when it fails. We can do this by developing those skills within our own team or by entering into relationships to help us. The larger our team and the more we rely on the component in question, the more likely it is that we should have some in-house expertise. The smaller our team and the less important the component, the more willing we should be to outsource the expertise. But in relying on partners for help, the relationship needs to go beyond that provided by most suppliers of equipment. The provider of the service needs to have "skin in the game." Put another way, they need to feel your pain and the pain of the customer when your service fails. You can't be caught in a wait queue for second level support while your customers scream at you for service restoration.

Summary

This chapter is a mix of rules that don't fit well in other chapters but are extremely important. Starting with a warning to avoid letting vendors provide scalability solutions through their products and continuing with advice about keeping business logic in the most appropriate place, monitoring appropriately, and finally being competent, we covered a wide variety of topics. While all of these rules are important perhaps no other rule than Rule 50, "Be Competent," brings it all together. Understanding and implementing these 50 rules is a great way to ensure that you and your team are competent when it comes to ensuring that your systems will scale.

Endnotes

1. "Gartner: Global Technology Spending Likely to Increase 33% in 2010," TOPNEWS, http://topnews.us/content/27798-gartner-global-technology-spending-likely-increase-33-2010.

2. That the data is unlikely to have occurred because of chance. Wikipedia, "Statistical significance," http://en.wikipedia.org/wiki/Statistical_significance.

13

Rule Review and Prioritization

In addition to being a handy aggregation of the rules for future reference, this chapter introduces a method by which these rules may be analyzed for application in your architecture. If you are building something from scratch, we highly recommend the inclusion of as many of the 50 rules as makes sense in your product. If you are attempting to redesign your existing system in an evolutionary fashion for greater scale, the method of risk-benefit analysis represented herein may help you prioritize the application of these rules in your reengineering efforts.

A Risk–Benefit Model for Evaluating Scalability Projects and Initiatives

Before we begin describing a risk-benefit model, let's first review why we are interested in scalability. The desire to have a highly available and usable (to some specified or implied quality of service metric) product or service, even under conditions of moderate to extreme growth, is why we invest in making our product scalable. If we weren't interested in what would happen to our product's availability or quality of service as demand increased on our site, we wouldn't be interested in attempting to scale it. This is the approach we think that most state governments take in implementing their Department of Motor Vehicles services. The government simply doesn't appear to care that people will line up and wait for hours during periods of peak demand. Nor do they care that the individuals providing service couldn't care less about the customer. The government knows it offers a service that customers must use if they want to drive and any customers who are dissatisfied and leave will simply come back another day. But most of the products that we build won't have this state sanctioned and protected monopoly. As a result, we must be concerned about our availability and hence our scalability.

It is within this context of concern over availability and scalability that we represent our concept of risk. The risk of an incident caused by the inability to scale manifests itself as a threat to our quality of service or availability. One method of calculating risk is to look at the probability that a problem will happen multiplied by its impact should it happen (or move from risk to issue). Figure 13.1 shows this method of risk decomposition.

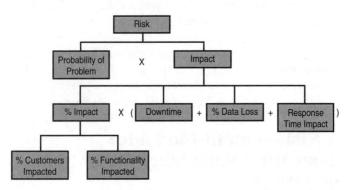

Figure 13.1   Scalability and availability risk
composition

The impact might be further broken down into components of the percentage impact to your user base and the actual impact such as downtime (the amount of time your service is unavailable), data loss, and response time degradation. Percentage impact might be further broken down into the percentage of the customers impacted and the percentage of the functionality impacted. There is certainly further decomposition possible; for instance, some customers may represent significantly greater value on either a license or transaction fee basis. Furthermore, downtime may have a different multiplier applied to it than response time; data loss may trump both of these.

This model isn't meant to hold true for all businesses. Rather it is meant to demonstrate a way in which you can build a model to help determine which things you should focus on in your business. One quick note before we proceed with how to use the model: We highly recommend that businesses calculate actual impact to revenue when determining the system's actual availability rather than attempting to model it as we've done here. For instance, if you can show or believe that you lost 10% of your expected revenue in a given day you should say your availability was 90%. Wall clock time is a terrible measure of availability as it treats every hour of every day equivalently, and most businesses don't have an equal distribution of traffic or revenue producing transactions. Now back to our regularly scheduled show.

The terminal nodes (nodes without children) of the decomposition graph of Figure 13.1 are leaves within our risk tree: Probability of a Problem, % Customers Impacted, % Functionality Impacted, Downtime, % Data Loss, and Response time Impact. Looking at these leaves, we can see that many of our rules map to these leaves. For instance, Rule 1 is really about decreasing the probability of a problem happening by ensuring that the system is easily understood and therefore less likely to be problematic. It may also decrease downtime as the solution is likely to be easier to troubleshoot and resolve. Using a bit of subjective analysis, we may decide that this rule has a small (or low) benefit to impact and a medium change to the probability of a problem happening. The result of this may be that the rule has an overall medium impact to risk (low + medium = ~medium).

We want to take just a minute and discuss how we arrived at this conclusion. The answer is that we used a simple High (H), Medium (M), and Low (L) analysis. There's no rocket science here (nor "rocket surgery" depending on how you prefer to coin a phrase); we simply used our experiences on how the rule might apply to the tree we developed for our particular view of risk and scalability. So while the answer was largely subjective, it was informed by 70 years of combined experience within our partnership. While you can certainly invest in creating a more deterministic model, we are not convinced that it will yield significantly better results than having a team of smart people determine how these rules impact your risk.

We are now going to assume that a change in risk serves as a proxy for benefit. This is a fairly well understood concept within business, so we won't spend a great deal of time explaining it. Suffice it to say that if you can reduce your risk, you reduce the likelihood of a negative impact to your business and therefore increase the probability of achieving your goals. What we need to do now is determine the cost of this risk reduction. Once we know that, we can take our benefit (risk reduction) and subtract our costs to develop the solution. This combination creates a prioritization of work. We suggest a simple High, Medium, and Low for cost. High cost might be anything more than $10M for a very large company to more than $10K for a very small company. Low cost could be anything less than $1M for a very large company or verging on zero for a very small company. This is often derived from the cost of developer days. For example if your average developer's salary and benefits cost the business $100,000 per year, then each day a developer needs to work on a project, assuming ~250 days of work per year, you add $400 to the cost.

Our prioritization equation then becomes risk reduction minus cost equals priority or $(R - C = P)$. Table 13.1 shows how we computed the nine permutations of risk and cost and the resulting priority. The method we chose was simple. The benefit for any equation where risk and cost were equivalent was set to medium and the priority set to the midrange of 3. Where risk reduction was two levels higher than cost, the benefit was set to Very High, and the Priority set to 1. Where risk reduction was two levels lower than cost (Low Risk, High Cost) the benefit was set to Very Low, and priority set to 5. Differences of one were either Low (Risk Reduction Low and Cost Medium) with a priority score of 4 or High (Risk Reduction Medium and Cost Low) with a priority score of 2. The projects with the lowest

priority score have the highest benefit and are the first things we
will do.

Table 13.1   **Risk Reduction, Cost, and Benefit Calculation**

Risk Reduction	Cost	Resulting Benefit/Priority
High	High	Medium 3
High	Medium	High 2
High	Low	Very High 1
Medium	High	Low 4
Medium	Medium	Medium 3
Medium	Low	High 2
Low	High	Very Low 5
Low	Medium	Low 4
Low	Low	Medium 3

Using the previous approach, we now rate each of our 50 rules.
The sidebars from each chapter for each rule are repeated in the
following sections with the addition of our estimation of risk
reduction, cost, and the calculated benefit/priority. As we mentioned earlier the way we arrived at these values was the result
of our experience of more than 70 years (combined) with more
than 150 companies and growing. Your particular risk reduction,
cost, and benefit may vary, and we encourage you to calculate
and prioritize these yourselves. Our estimates should be good for
smaller action-oriented companies that simply want to know
what to do today. Note that these estimates are to "rework" an
existing solution. The cost of designing something from scratch
will be significantly different—typically a lower cost but with
equivalent benefit.

For the sake of completeness, there are many other approaches to determining cost and benefit. You may, for instance, replace
our notion of risk reduction with the ability to achieve specific
KPIs (Key Performance Indicators) within your company. The
previous method would be appropriate if you had a KPI regarding the scalability and availability of your product (something all
Web-enabled businesses should have). If you are a business with
contractual obligations another approach might be to determine
the risk reduction of not meeting specific SLAs (Service Level

Agreements) outlined within your contracts. Many other possibilities exist. Just choose the right approach to prioritize for your
business and get going!

Rule 1—Don't Overengineer the Solution

What: Guard against complex solutions during design.
When to use: Can be used for any project and should be used
for all large or complex systems or projects.
How to use: Resist the urge to overengineer solutions by
testing ease of understanding with fellow engineers.
Why: Complex solutions are costly to implement and have
excessive long-term costs.
Risk reduction: M
Cost: L
Benefit and priority: High - 2
Key takeaways: Systems that are overly complex limit your
ability to scale. Simple systems are more easily and cost
effectively maintained and scaled.

Rule 2—Design Scale into the Solution (D-I-D Process)

What: An approach to provide JIT (Just In Time) Scalability.
When to use: On all projects; this approach is the most cost-
effective (resources and time) to ensure scalability.
How to use:

- Design for 20x capacity.
- Implement for 3x capacity.
- Deploy for ~1.5x capacity.

Why: D-I-D provides a cost-effective, JIT method of scaling
your product.
Risk reduction: L
Cost: L
Benefit and priority: Medium - 3
Key takeaways: Teams can save a lot of money and time by
thinking of how to scale solutions early, implementing (coding)
them a month or so before they are needed, and implementing
them days before the customer rush or demand.

Rule 3—Simplify the Solution 3 Times Over

What: Used when designing complex systems, this rule simplifies the scope, design, and implementation.

When to use: When designing complex systems or products where resources (engineering or computational) are limited.

How to use:

- Simplify scope using the Pareto principle.

- Simplify design by thinking about cost-effectiveness and scalability.

- Simplify implementation by leveraging the experience of others.

Why: Focusing just on "not being complex" doesn't address the issues created in requirements or story and epoch development or the actual implementation.

Risk reduction: L

Cost: L

Benefit and priority: Medium - 3

Key takeaways: Simplification needs to happen during every aspect of product development.

Rule 4—Reduce DNS Lookups

What: Reduce the number of DNS lookups from a user perspective.

When to use: On all Web pages where performance matters.

How to use: Minimize the number of DNS lookups required to download pages, but balance this with the browser's limitation for simultaneous connections.

Why: DNS lookups take a great deal of time, and large numbers of them can amount to a large portion of your user experience.

Risk reduction: L

Cost: L

Benefit and priority: Medium - 3

Key takeaways: Reduction of objects, tasks, computation, and so on is a great way of speeding up page load time, but division of labor must be considered as well.

Rule 5—Reduce Objects Where Possible

What: Reduce the number of objects on a page where possible.
When to use: On all Web pages where performance matters.
How to use:

- Reduce or combine objects, but balance this with maximizing simultaneous connections.
- Test changes to ensure performance improvements.

Why: The number of objects impacts page download times.
Risk reduction: L
Cost: L
Benefit and priority: Medium – 3
Key takeaways: The balance between objects and methods that serve them is a science that requires constant measurement and adjustment; it's a balance between customer usability, usefulness, and performance.

Rule 6—Use Homogenous Networks

What: Don't mix the vendor networking gear.
When to use: When designing or expanding your network.
How to use:

- Do not mix different vendors' networking gear (switches and routers).
- Buy best of breed for other networking gear (firewalls, load balancers, and so on).

Why: Intermittent interoperability and availability issues simply aren't worth the potential cost savings.
Risk reduction: H
Cost: H
Benefit and priority: Medium – 3
Key takeaways: Heterogeneous networking gear tends to cause availability and scalability problems. Choose a single provider.

Rule 7—Design to Clone Things (X Axis)

What: Typically called horizontal scale, this is the duplication of services or databases to spread transaction load.

When to use:

- Databases with a very high read to write ratio (5:1 or greater—the higher the better).

- Any system where transaction growth exceeds data growth.

How to use:

- Simply clone services and implement a load balancer.

- For databases, ensure the accessing code understands the difference between a read and a write.

Why: Allows for fast scale of transactions at the cost of duplicated data and functionality.

Risk reduction: M

Cost: L

Benefit and priority: High - 2

Key takeaways: X axis splits are fast to implement and can allow for transaction but not data scalability.

Rule 8—Design to Split Different Things (Y Axis)

What: Sometimes referred to as scale through services or resources, this rule focuses on scaling data sets, transactions, and engineering teams.

When to use:

- Very large data sets where relations between data are not necessary.

- Large, complex systems where scaling engineering resources require specialization.

How to use:

- Split up actions by using verbs or resources by using nouns or use a mix.

- Split both the services and the data along the lines defined by the verb/noun approach.

Why: Allows for efficient scaling of not only transactions but also very large data sets associated with those transactions.

Risk reduction: M
Cost: M
Benefit and priority: Medium – 3
Key takeaways: Y axis or data/service-oriented splits, allow for efficient scaling of transactions, large data sets, and can help with fault isolation.

Rule 9—Design to Split Similar Things (Z Axis)

What: This is often a split by some unique aspect of the customer such as customer ID, name, geography, and so on.
When to use: Very large, similar data sets such as large and rapidly growing customer bases.
How to use: Identify something you know about the customer, such as customer ID, last name, geography, or device and split or partition both data and services based on that attribute.
Why: Rapid customer growth exceeds other forms of data growth or you have the need to perform "fault isolation" between certain customer groups as you scale.
Risk reduction: H
Cost: H
Benefit and priority: Medium – 3
Key takeaways: Z axis splits are effective at helping you to scale customer bases but can also be applied to other very large data sets that can't be pulled apart using the Y axis methodology.

Rule 10—Design Your Solution to Scale Out—Not Just Up

What: *Scaling out* is the duplication of services or databases to spread transaction load and is the alternative to buying larger hardware, known as *scaling up*.
When to use: Any system, service, or database expected to grow rapidly.
How to use: Use the AKF Scale Cube to determine the correct split for your environment. Usually the horizontal split (cloning) is the easiest.
Why: Allows for fast scale of transactions at the cost of duplicated data and functionality.

Risk reduction: M
Cost: L
Benefit and priority: High - 2
Key takeaways: Plan for success and design your systems to scale out. Don't get caught in the trap of expecting to scale up only to find out that you've run out of faster and larger systems to purchase.

Rule 11—Use Commodity Systems (Goldfish Not Thoroughbreds)

What: Use small, inexpensive systems where possible.
When to use: Use this approach in your production environment when going through hyper growth.
How to use: Stay away from very large systems in your production environment.
Why: Allows for fast, cost-effective growth.
Risk reduction: M
Cost: L
Benefit and priority: High - 2
Key takeaways: Build your systems to be capable of relying on commodity hardware and don't get caught in the trap of using high margin, high end servers.

Rule 12—Scale Out Your Data Centers

What: Design your systems to have three or more live data centers to reduce overall cost, increase availability, and implement disaster recovery.
When to use: Any rapidly growing business that is considering adding a disaster recovery (cold site) data center.
How to use: Split up your data to spread across data centers and spread transaction load across those data centers in a "multiple live" configuration. Use spare capacity for peak periods of the year.
Why: The cost of data center failure can be disastrous to your business. Design to have three or more as the cost is often less than having two data centers. Make use of idle capacity for peak periods rather than slowing down your transactions.

Risk reduction: H
Cost: H
Benefit and priority: Medium - 3
Key takeaways: When implementing DR, lower your cost of disaster recovery by designing your systems to leverage three or more live data centers. Use the spare capacity for spiky demand when necessary.

Rule 13—Design to Leverage the Cloud

What: This is the purposeful utilization of cloud technologies to scale on demand.
When to use: When demand is temporary, spiky, and inconsistent and when response time is not a core issue in the product.
How to use:

- Make use of third-party cloud environments for temporary demands, such as large batch jobs or QA environments during testing cycles.

- Design your application to service some requests from a third-party cloud when demand exceeds a certain peak level.

Why: Provisioning of hardware in a cloud environment takes a few minutes as compared to days or weeks for physical servers in your own collocation facility. When utilized temporarily this is also very cost effective.
Risk reduction: L
Cost: M
Benefit and priority: Low - 4
Key takeaways: Design to leverage virtualization and the cloud to meet unexpected spiky demand.

Rule 14—Use Databases Appropriately

What: Use relational databases when you need ACID properties to maintain relationships between your data. For other data storage needs consider more appropriate tools.
When to use: When you are introducing new data or data structures into the architecture of a system.

How to use: Consider the data volume, amount of storage, response time requirements, relationships, and other factors to choose the most appropriate storage tool.

Why: RDBMSs provide great transactional integrity but are more difficult to scale, cost more, and have lower availability than many other storage options.

Risk reduction: M

Cost: L

Benefit and priority: High - 2

Key takeaways: Use the right storage tool for your data. Don't get lured into sticking everything in a relational database just because you are comfortable accessing data in a database.

Rule 15—Firewalls, Firewalls Everywhere!

What: Use firewalls only when they significantly reduce risk and recognize that they cause issues with scalability and availability.

When to use: Always.

How to use: Employ firewalls for critical PII, PCI compliance, and so on. Don't use them for low-value static content.

Why: Firewalls can lower availability and cause unnecessary scalability chokepoints.

Risk reduction: M

Cost: L

Benefit and priority: High - 2

Key takeaways: While firewalls are useful, they are often overused and represent both an availability and a scalability concern if not designed and implemented properly.

Rule 16—Actively Use Log Files

What: Use your application's log files to diagnose and prevent problems.

When to use: Put a process in place that monitors log files and forces people to take action on issues identified.

How to use: Use any number of monitoring tools from custom scripts to Splunk to watch your application logs for errors. Export these and assign resources for identifying and solving the issue.

Why: The log files are excellent sources of information about how your application is performing for your users; don't throw this resource away without using it.

Risk reduction: L

Cost: L

Benefit and priority: Medium – 3

Key takeaways: Make good use of your log files and you will have fewer production issues with your system.

Rule 17—Don't Check Your Work

What: Avoid checking things you just did or reading things you just wrote within your products.

When to use: Always (see rule conflict discussion in Rule 17 in Chapter 5).

How to use: Never read what you just wrote for the purpose of validation. Store data in a local or distributed cache if it is required for operations in the near future.

Why: The cost of validating your work is high relative to the unlikely cost of failure. Such activities run counter to cost-effective scaling.

Risk reduction: L

Cost: M

Benefit and priority: Low – 4

Key takeaways: Never justify reading something you just wrote for the purposes of validating the data. Read and act upon errors associated with the write activity instead. Avoid other types of reads of recently written data by storing that data locally.

Rule 18—Stop Redirecting Traffic

What: Avoid redirects when possible; use the right method when they are necessary.

When to use: Use redirects as little as possible.

How to use: If you must have them, consider server configurations instead of HTML or other code-based solutions.

Why: Redirects in general delay the user, consume computation resources, and are prone to errors.

Risk reduction: L

Cost: L

Benefit and priority: Medium - 3
Key Takeaways: Use redirect correctly and only when necessary.

Rule 19—Relax Temporal Constraints

What: Alleviate temporal constraints in your system whenever possible.
When to use: Anytime you are considering adding a constraint that an item or object maintains a certain state between a user's actions.
How to use: Relax constraints in the business rules.
Why: The difficulty in scaling systems with temporal constraints is significant because of the ACID properties of most RDMSs.
Risk reduction: H
Cost: L
Benefit and priority: Very High - 1
Key takeaways: Carefully consider the need for constraints such as items being available from the time a user views them until the user purchases them. Some possible edge cases where users are disappointed are much easier to compensate for than not being able to scale.

Rule 20—Leverage CDNs

What: Use CDNs to offload traffic from your site.
When to use: Ensure it is cost justified and then choose which content is most suitable.
How to use: Most CDNs leverage DNS to serve content on your site's behalf.
Why: CDNs help offload traffic spikes and are often economical ways to scale parts of a site's traffic.
Risk reduction: M
Cost: M
Benefit and priority: Medium - 3
Key takeaways: CDNs are a fast and simple way to offset spikiness of traffic as well as traffic growth in general. Ensure you perform a cost-benefit analysis and monitor the CDN usage.

Rule 21—Use Expires Headers

What: Use Expires headers to reduce requests and improve the scalability and performance of your system.

When to use: All object types need to be considered.

How to use: Headers can be set on Web servers or through application code.

Why: The reduction of object requests increases the page performance for the user and decreases the number of requests your system must handle per user.

Risk reduction: L

Cost: L

Benefit and priority: Medium – 3

Key takeaways: For each object type (image, html, css, php, and so on) consider how long the object can be cached for and implement the appropriate header for that timeframe.

Rule 22—Cache Ajax Calls

What: Use appropriate HTTP response headers to ensure cacheability of Ajax calls.

When to use: Every Ajax call but those absolutely requiring real time data that is likely to have been recently updated.

How to use: Modify Last-Modified, Cache-Control, and Expires headers appropriately.

Why: Decrease user-perceived response time, increase user satisfaction, and increase the scalability of your platform or solution.

Risk reduction: M

Cost: L

Benefit and priority: High – 2

Key takeaways: Leverage Ajax and cache Ajax calls as much as possible to increase user satisfaction and increase scalability.

Rule 23—Leverage Page Caches

What: Deploy Page Caches in front of your Web services.

When to use: Always.

How to use: Choose a caching system and deploy.

Why: Decrease load on Web servers by caching and delivering previously generated dynamic requests and quickly answering calls for static objects.

Risk reduction: M
Cost: M
Benefit and priority: Medium – 3
Key takeaways: Page caches are a great way to offload dynamic requests and to scale cost effectively.

Rule 24—Utilize Application Caches

What: Alleviate temporal constraints in your system whenever possible.
When to use: Anytime you are considering adding a constraint that an item or object maintains a certain state between a user's actions.
How to use: Relax constraints in the business rules.
Why: The difficulty in scaling systems with temporal constraints is significant because of the ACID properties of most RDMSs.
Risk reduction: M
Cost: M
Benefit and priority: Medium – 3
Key takeaways: Carefully consider the need for constraints such as items being available from the time a user views it until the user purchases it. Some possible edge cases where users are disappointed are much easier to compensate for than not being able to scale.

Rule 25—Make Use of Object Caches

What: Implement object caches to help your system scale.
When to use: Anytime you have repetitive queries or computations.
How to use: Select any one of the many open source or vendor supported solutions and implement the calls in your application code.
Why: A fairly straightforward object cache implementation can save a lot of computational resources on application servers or database servers.
Risk reduction: H
Cost: L
Benefit and priority: Very High – 1

Key takeaways: Consider implementing an object cache anywhere computations are performed repeatedly, but primarily this is done between the database and application tiers.

Rule 26—Put Object Caches on Their Own "Tier"

What: Use a separate tier in your architecture for object caches.
When to use: Anytime you have implemented object caches.
How to use: Move object caches onto their own servers.
Why: The benefits of a separate tier are better utilization of memory and CPU resources and having the ability to scale the object cache independently of other tiers.
Risk reduction: M
Cost: L
Benefit and priority: High – 2
Key takeaways: When implementing an object cache it is simplest to put the service on an existing tier such as the application servers. Consider implementing or moving the object cache to its own tier for better performance and scalability.

Rule 27—Learn Aggressively

What: Take every opportunity to learn.
When to use: Be constantly learning from your mistakes as well as successes.
How to use: Watch your customers or use A/B testing to determine what works. Use postmortems to learn from incidents and problems in production.
Why: Doing something without measuring the results or having an incident without learning from it are wasted opportunities that your competitors are taking advantage of.
Risk reduction: M
Cost: L
Benefit and priority: High – 2
Key takeaways: Be constantly and aggressively learning. The companies that do this best are the ones that grow the fastest and are the most scalable.

Rule 28—Don't Rely on QA to Find Mistakes

What: Use QA to lower cost of delivered products, increase engineering throughput, identify quality trends, and decrease defects—*not* to increase quality.

When to use: Whenever you can get greater throughput by hiring someone focused on testing rather than writing code. Use QA to learn from past mistakes—always.

How to use: Hire a QA person anytime you get greater than one engineer's worth of output with the hiring of a single QA person.

Why: Reduce cost, increase delivery volume/velocity, and decrease the number of repeated defects.

Risk reduction: M

Cost: L

Benefit and priority: High - 2

Key takeaways: QA doesn't increase the quality of your system, as you can't test quality into a system. If used properly, it can increase your productivity while decreasing cost, and most importantly it can keep you from increasing defect rates faster than your rate of organization growth during periods of rapid hiring.

Rule 29—Failing to Design for Rollback Is Designing for Failure

What: Always have the ability to roll back code.

When to use: Ensure all releases have the ability to roll back, practice it in a staging or QA environment, and use it in production when necessary to resolve customer incidents.

How to use: Clean up your code and follow a few simple procedures to ensure you can roll back your code.

Why: If you haven't experienced the pain of not being able to roll back, you likely will at some point if you keep playing with the "fix-forward" fire.

Risk reduction: H

Cost: L

Benefit and priority: Very High - 1

Key takeaways: Don't accept that the application is too complex or that you release code too often as excuses that you can't roll back. No sane pilot would take off in an airplane without the ability to land, and no sane engineer would roll code that they could not pull back off in an emergency.

Rule 30—Discuss and Learn from Failures

What: Leverage every failure to learn and teach important lessons.
When to use: Always.
How to use: Employ a postmortem process and hypothesize failures in low failure environments.
Why: We learn best from our mistakes—not our successes.
Risk reduction: H
Cost: L
Benefit and priority: Very High - 1
Key takeaways: Never let a good failure go to waste. Learn from every one and identify the technology, people, and process issues that need to be corrected.

Rule 31—Be Aware of Costly Relationships

What: Be aware of relationships in the data model.
When to use: When designing the data model, adding tables/columns, or writing queries consider how the relationships between entities will affect performance and scalability in the long run.
How to use: Think about database splits and possible future data needs as you design the data model.
Why: The cost of fixing a broken data model after it has been implemented is likely 100x as much as fixing it during the design phase.
Risk reduction: L
Cost: L
Benefit and priority: Medium - 3
Key takeaways: Think ahead and plan the data model carefully. Consider normalized forms, how you will likely split the database in the future, and possible data needs of the application.

Rule 32—Use the Right Type of Database Lock

What: Be cognizant of the use of explicit locks and monitor implicit locks.

When to use: Anytime you employ relational databases for your solution.

How to use: Monitor explicit locks in code reviews. Monitor databases for implicit locks and adjust explicitly as necessary to moderate throughput. Choose a database and storage engine that allows flexibility in types and granularity of locking.

Why: Maximize concurrency and throughput in databases within your environment.

Risk reduction: H

Cost: L

Benefit and priority: Very High - 1

Key takeaways: Understand the types of locks and manage their usage to maximize database throughput and concurrency. Change lock types to get better utilization of databases and look to split schemas or distribute databases as you grow. When choosing databases, ensure you choose one that allows multiple lock types and granularity to maximize concurrency.

Rule 33—Pass on Using Multiphase Commits

What: Do not use a multiphase commit protocol to store or process transactions.

When to use: Always pass, or alternatively never use multiphase commits.

How to use: Don't use it; split your data storage and processing systems with Y or Z axis splits.

Why: Multiphase commits are blocking protocols that do not permit other transactions from occurring until it is complete.

Risk reduction: M

Cost: L

Benefit and priority: High - 2

Key takeaways: Do not use multiphase commit protocols as a simple way to extend the life of your monolithic database. It will likely cause it to scale even less and result in an even earlier demise of your system.

Rule 34—Try Not to Use "Select For Update"

What: Minimize the use of the FOR UPDATE clause in a SELECT statement when declaring cursors.
When to use: Always.
How to use: Review cursor development and question every SELECT FOR UPDATE usage.
Why: Use of FOR UPDATE causes locks on rows and may slow down transactions.
Risk reduction: M
Cost: L
Benefit and priority: High - 2
Key takeaways: Cursors are powerful constructs that when properly used can actually make programming faster and easier while speeding up transactions. But FOR UPDATE cursors may cause long held locks and slow transactions. Refer to your database documentation for whether you need to use the FOR READ ONLY clause to minimize locks.

Rule 35—Don't Select Everything

What: Don't use Select * in queries.
When to use: Never select everything (unless of course you are going to use everything).
How to use: Always declare what columns of data you are selecting or inserting in a query.
Why: Selecting everything in a query is prone to break things when the table structure changes and it transfers unneeded data.
Risk reduction: H
Cost: L
Benefit and priority: Very High - 1
Key takeaways: Don't use wildcards when selecting or inserting data.

Rule 36—Design Using Fault Isolative "Swimlanes"

What: Implement fault isolation or "swimlanes" in your designs.
When to use: Whenever you are beginning to split up databases to scale.

How to use: Split up databases and services along the Y or Z axis and disallow synchronous communication or access between services.

Why: Increase availability, scalability, and reduce incident identification and resolution as well as time to market and cost.

Risk reduction: H

Cost: H

Benefit and priority: Medium - 3

Key takeaways: Fault isolation consists of eliminating synchronous calls between fault isolation domains, limiting asynchronous calls and handling synchronous call failure, and eliminating the sharing of services and data between swimlanes.

Rule 37—Never Trust Single Points of Failure

What: Never implement and always eliminate single points of failure.

When to use: During architecture reviews and new designs.

How to use: Identify single instances on architectural diagrams. Strive for active/active configurations.

Why: Maximize availability through multiple instances.

Risk reduction: H

Cost: M

Benefit and priority: High - 2

Key takeaways: Strive for active/active rather than active/passive solutions. Use load balancers to balance traffic across instances of a service. Use control services with active/passive instances for patterns that require singletons.

Rule 38—Avoid Putting Systems in Series

What: Reduce the number of components that are connected in series.

When to use: Anytime you are considering adding components.

How to use: Remove unnecessary components or add multiple versions of them to minimize the impact.

Why: Components in series have a multiplicative effect of failure.

Risk reduction: M

Cost: M
Benefit and priority: Medium – 3
Key takeaways: Avoid adding components to your system that are connected in series. When necessary to do so add multiple versions of that component so that if one fails others are available to take its place.

Rule 39—Ensure You Can Wire On and Off Functions

What: Create a framework to disable and enable features of your product.
When to use: Risky, very high use, or shared services that might otherwise cause site failures when slow to respond or unavailable.
How to use: Develop shared libraries to allow automatic or on-demand enabling and disabling of services. See Table 9.4 for recommendations.
Why: Graceful failure (or handling failures) of transactions can keep you in business while you recover from the incident and problem that caused it.
Risk reduction: M
Cost: H
Benefit and priority: Low – 4
Key takeaways: Implement Wire On/Wire Off frameworks whenever the cost of implementation is less than the risk and associated cost of failure. Work to develop shared libraries that can be reused to lower the cost of future implementation.

Rule 40—Strive for Statelessness

What: Design and implement stateless systems.
When to use: During design of new systems and redesign of existing systems.
How to use: Choose stateless implementations whenever possible. If stateful implementations are warranted for business reasons, refer to Rules 41 and 42.
Why: The implementation of state limits scalability and increases cost.
Risk reduction: H

Cost: H
Benefit and priority: Medium – 3
Key takeaways: Always push back on the need for state in any system. Use business metrics and multivariate (or A/B) testing to determine whether state in an application truly results in the expected user behavior and business value.

Rule 41—Maintain Sessions in the Browser When Possible

What: Try to avoid session data completely, but when needed, consider putting the data in users' browsers.
When to use: Anytime that you need session data for the best user experience.
How to use: Use cookies to store session data on the users' browsers.
Why: Keeping session data on the users' browsers allows the user request to be served by any Web server in the pool and takes the storage requirement away from your system.
Risk reduction: M
Cost: L
Benefit and priority: High – 2
Key takeaways: Using cookies to store session data is a common approach and has advantages in terms of ease of scale but also has some drawbacks. One of the most critical cons is that unsecured cookies can easily be captured and used to log into people's accounts.

Rule 42—Make Use of a Distributed Cache for States

What: Use a distributed cache when storing session data in your system.
When to use: Anytime you need to store session data and cannot do so in users' browsers.
How to use: Watch for some common mistakes such as a session management system that requires affinity of a user to a Web server.
Why: Careful consideration of how to store session data can help ensure your system will continue to scale.

Risk reduction: M
Cost: L
Benefit and priority: High – 2
Key takeaways: Many Web servers or languages offer simple server-based session management, but these are often fraught with problems such as user affiliation with specific servers. Implementing a distributed cache will allow you to store session data in your system and continue to scale.

Rule 43—Communicate Asynchronously As Much As Possible

What: Use asynchronous instead of synchronous communication as often as possible.
When to use: Consider for all calls between services and tiers.
How to use: Use language-specific calls to ensure the requests are made and not waited on.
Why: Synchronous calls stop the entire program's execution waiting for a response, which ties all the services and tiers together resulting in cascading failures.
Risk reduction: H
Cost: M
Benefit and priority: High – 2
Key takeaways: Use asynchronous communication techniques to ensure that each service and tier is as independent as possible. This allows the system to scale much farther than if all components are closely coupled together.

Rule 44—Ensure Your Message Bus Can Scale

What: Message buses can fail from demand like any other physical or logical system. They need to be scaled.
When to use: Anytime a message bus is part of your architecture.
How to use: Employ the Y and Z AKF axes of scale.
Why: To ensure your bus scales to demand.
Risk reduction: H
Cost: M
Benefit and priority: High – 2

Key takeaways: Treat message buses like any other critical component of your system. Scale them ahead of demand using either the Y or Z axes of scale.

Rule 45—Avoid Overcrowding Your Message Bus

What: Limit bus traffic to items of higher value than the cost to handle them.

When to use: On any message bus.

How to use: Value and cost justify message traffic. Eliminate low value, high cost traffic. Sample low value/low cost and high value/high cost traffic to reduce the cost.

Why: Message traffic isn't "free" and presents costly demand on your system.

Risk reduction: M

Cost: L

Benefit and priority: High - 2

Key takeaways: Don't publish everything. Sample traffic to ensure alignment between cost and value.

Rule 46—Be Wary of Scaling Through Third Parties

What: Scale your own system; don't rely on vendor solutions to achieve scalability.

When to use: When considering whether to use a new feature or product from a vendor.

How to use: Rely on the rules of this book for understanding how to scale and use vendor provided products and services in the most simplistic manner possible.

Why: Three reasons for following this rule: Own your destiny, keep your architecture simple, and reduce your total cost of ownership.

Risk reduction: H

Cost: L

Benefit and priority: Very High - 1

Key takeaways: Do not rely on vendor products, services, or features to scale your system. Keep your architecture simple, keep your destiny in your own hands, and keep your costs in control. All three of these can be violated by using a vendor's proprietary scaling solution.

Rule 47—Purge, Archive, and Cost-Justify Storage

What: Match storage cost to data value, including removing data of value lower than the costs to store it.

When to use: Apply to data and its underlying storage infrastructure during design discussions and throughout the lifecycle of the data in question.

How to use: Apply recency, frequency, and monetization analysis to determine the value of the data. Match storage costs to data value.

Why: Not all data is created equal (that is, of the same value) and in fact it often changes in value over time. Why then should we have a single storage solution with equivalent cost for that data?

Risk reduction: M

Cost: M

Benefit and priority: Medium – 3

Key takeaways: It is important to understand and calculate the value of your data and to match storage costs to that value. Don't pay for data that doesn't have a stakeholder return.

Rule 48—Remove Business Intelligence from Transaction Processing

What: Separate business systems from product systems and product intelligence from database systems.

When to use: Anytime you are considering internal company needs and data transfer within, to, or from your product.

How to use: Remove stored procedures from the database and put them in your application logic. Do not make synchronous calls between corporate and product systems.

Why: Putting application logic in databases is costly and represents scale challenges. Tying corporate systems and product systems together is also costly and represents similar scale challenges as well as availability concerns.

Risk reduction: H

Cost: M

Benefit and priority: High – 2

Key takeaways: Databases and internal corporate systems can be costly to scale due to license and unique system characteristics. As such, we want them dedicated to their specific tasks. In the cases of databases, we want them focused on transactions rather than product intelligence. In the case of back office systems (business intelligence), we do not want our product tied to their capabilities to scale. Use asynchronous transfer of data for business systems.

Rule 49—Design Your Application to Be Monitored

What: Think about how you will need to monitor your application as you are designing it.

When to use: Anytime you are adding or changing modules of your code base.

How to use: Build hooks into your system to record transaction times.

Why: Having insight into how your application is performing will help answer many questions when there is a problem.

Risk reduction: M

Cost: L

Benefit and priority: High – 2

Key takeaways: Adopt as an architectural principle that your application must be monitored. Additionally, look at your overall monitoring strategy to make sure you are first answering the question of "Is there a problem?" and then the "Where" and "What."

Rule 50—Be Competent

What: Be competent, or buy competency in/for each component of your architecture.

When to use: For any Internet service or commerce solution.

How to use: For each component of your infrastructure, identify the team responsible and level of competency with that component.

Why: To a customer, every problem is *your* problem. You can't blame suppliers or providers. You provide a service—not software.

Risk reduction: H

Cost: L

Benefit and priority: Very High - 1

Key takeaways: Don't confuse competence with build versus buy or core versus context decisions. You can buy solutions and still be competent in their deployment and maintenance. In fact, your customers demand that you do so.

A Benefit/Priority Ranking of the Scalability Rules

As you would expect the distribution of rules is fairly normal but shifted toward the high end of benefit and priority. There are of course no rules that were ranked Very Low since they would not have made the cut for inclusion in the list. The following sections group the 50 rules by Benefit/Priority for ease of reference.

Very High – 1

Rule 19	Relax Temporal Constraints
Rule 25	Make Use of Object Caches
Rule 29	Failing to Design for Rollback Is Designing for Failure
Rule 30	Discuss and Learn from Failures
Rule 32	Use the Right Type of Database Lock
Rule 35	Don't Select Everything
Rule 46	Be Wary of Scaling Through Third Parties
Rule 50	Be Competent

High – 2

Medium – 3

Rule 18	Stop Redirecting Traffic
Rule 20	Leverage CDNs
Rule 21	Use Expires Headers
Rule 23	Leverage Page Caches
Rule 24	Utilize Application Caches
Rule 31	Be Aware of Costly Relationships
Rule 36	Design Using Fault Isolative "Swimlanes"
Rule 38	Avoid Putting Systems in Series
Rule 40	Strive for Statelessness
Rule 47	Purge, Archive, and Cost-Justify Storage

Low – 4

Rule 13	Design to Leverage the Cloud
Rule 17	Don't Check Your Work
Rule 39	Ensure You Can Wire On and Off Functions

Very Low – 5

N/A

Summary

This chapter was a summary of the 50 rules in this book. Additionally we provided a method by which these rules can be prioritized for a generic Web-based business looking to re-architect its platform in an evolutionary fashion. The prioritization does not mean as much for a business just starting to build its product or platform because it is much easier to build in many of these rules at relatively low cost when you are building something from scratch.

As with any rule there are exceptions, and not all of these rules will apply to your specific technology endeavors. For instance, you may not employ traditional relational databases in which case our database rules will not apply to you. In some cases, it does not make sense to implement or employ a rule due to cost constraints and the uncertainty of your business. After all, as many of our rules imply, you don't want to overcomplicate your solution, and you want to incur costs at an appropriate time so as to maintain profitability. Rule 2 is a recognition of this need to scale cost effectively; where you can't afford the time or money to implement a solution today, at least spend some amount of comparatively cheap time deciding how the solution will look when you do implement it. One example might be to wait to implement a scalable (fault isolated and Y or Z axis scaled) message bus. If you don't implement the solution in code and systems infrastructure, you should at least discuss how you will make such an implementation in the future if your business becomes successful.

Similarly there are exceptions with our method of prioritizing these rules. We have applied a repeatable model that encapsulates our collective learning across many companies. Because the result is, in a fashion, an average, it is subject to the same problem as all averages: In attempting to describe an entire population it is going to be wrong for many specific data points. Feel free to modify our mechanism to fit your specific needs.

A great use for this chapter is to select a number of rules that fit your specific needs and codify them as architectural principles within your organization. Use these principles as the standards employed within software and infrastructure reviews. The exit criteria for these meetings can be complete adherence to the set of rules that you develop. Architectural reviews and joint architectural development sessions can similarly employ these rules to ensure adherence to principles of scalability and availability.

Whether your system is still in the design phase on the whiteboard or ten years old with millions of lines of code, incorporating these rules into your architecture will help improve its scalability. If you're an engineer or an architect, make use of these rules in your designs. If you are a manager or an executive, share these rules with your teams. We wish you the best of luck with all your scalability projects.

Index

FREE Online Edition

Your purchase of **Scalability Rules** includes access to a free online edition for 45 days through the Safari Books Online subscription service. Nearly every Addison-Wesley Professional book is available online through Safari Books Online, along with more than 5,000 other technical books and videos from publishers such as Cisco Press, Exam Cram, IBM Press, O'Reilly, Prentice Hall, Que, and Sams.

SAFARI BOOKS ONLINE allows you to search for a specific answer, cut and paste code, download chapters, and stay current with emerging technologies.

Activate your FREE Online Edition at www.informit.com/safarifree

> **STEP 1:** Enter the coupon code: HNMNVFA.

> **STEP 2:** New Safari users, complete the brief registration form. Safari subscribers, just log in.

If you have difficulty registering on Safari or accessing the online edition, please e-mail customer-service@ safaribooksonline.com

Safari
Books Online